I first of all want to give thanks to universal law for giving me the vibrations to complete that which I begun. I also give thanks to my parents whose reactions forged my construction. My Mother for doing what she needed to. My father for doing what he didn't have to. I'd like to thank every woman that has ever been in my life, most of which have been the true motivation of my written pain. I'd like to thank the poetic community, exclusively the poets and fans of poetry from the internet community. Without you my Spirit could have never been Wild enough to write this book. I want to thank every fan of the Breathing Through Paper show and all the poets who were willing to wake up late for work on Friday to hang with us, thank you. I have to thank my Grandmother for keeping her blessed hands on me … praying on me till the day she died. I love you always Grandma. I want to thank Envy_Seal and all of Pleasure Principle Publications for taking a leap of faith and giving me this opportunity, I truly can't thank you enough. Lastly but just as importantly I want to thank you. For being a supporter of my work; or for just looking at the cover and saying "let me see what this guy talkin' about". I know money tight nowadays so I really appreciate your purchase.

Thank you

WrittenInPa

Conversations With Myself

By: WrittenInPain

INTRODUCTION

I wrote my first poem when I was around five or six years old. I guess you could consider it a poem, when I was very young my mother bought me the "Dr. Seuss" series that's where I fell in love with rhyme schemes. I would often try to compile whole stories using rhyme schemes. (Often sequels to already existing Dr. Seuss stories) My addiction for Dr. Suess made reading everything else lame; honestly I absolutely hated the Berenstain Bears because of the lack of cadence. So anyway by six I wrote my first poem.

"I am not a killer
Uncle Kim drinks Miller
Michael Jackson is a Thriller
My name is Carlos"

By all means in my mind it was a masterpiece. I read this so many times it burned into my memory. (Obviously) Everyone liked it, the first thirty times only my grandmother liked it EVERY time. But that was it; at six I had mastered the art of poetry. I had moved on to bigger things, like Pac-man and figuring out this damn Rubix cube. I still kept reading Dr. Seuss most likely until I was too old to. In fact if I'm some place and I see "Fox in Sox" lying around or "Green eggs and Ham" No lie I'm a give it a flip.

I grew up in the South Bronx which is credited for being the birth place of Hip Hop; I remember my mother wouldn't let me listen to it. But it was the soundtrack of the streets, the culture the feel was everywhere. By the time I was in Junior High school it had exploded and everybody was trying to be an Mc or a Dj. For me… it was the rhyme schemes, the cadence the word play. It wasn't like now; rappers were not these bigger than life people that seemed so far away. You would see Nice & Smooth in the street everybody in Harlem knew Biz Markie and it was nothing to ride a train and see a gang of kids circling two who were flinging words at each other. I remember using whole lunch periods to craft something on paper for my after school battles. It was never enough; if you were from the BX (the Bronx) your freestyle had to be on point. I earned a name for myself in some circles at this point. It was Hip Hop that transformed me into an obsessive writer. I could not possibly get my mind around how much writing I did during that time but it was fundamentally the era a honed in on whatever it is I do now. It was also Hip Hop that introduced me to poetry. Some teenagers at a talent show had performed their Hip Hop rendition of The Raven, it was horrible but it made me want to read the real poem. So between putting them bars together I would read Poe, Yates, Frost few others. But I was a Poe fan to the heart.

Eventually Hip Hop would break my heart as an aspiring rap career turned into a string of empty promises. Soon after I stopped writing Rap songs, I stopped writing all together. Hip Hop had disappointed me so much I really didn't listen to it as much. This is when I discovered Prince. I had known who he was already Purple Rain dude with the questionable wardrobe but I was a Michael Jackson fan like the rest of the world so that was that. But my Father would play these records Pop Life, America and Sign o' the Times. In my opinion these songs were poems to music; his range in writing was his true genius to me. God, Irresistible Bitch and I wanna be your lover all came from the same mind. It was funny to me in High School while everyone else was listening to Black Sheep, N.W.A and Snoop I would have the "Under the Cherry Moon" soundtrack pumping in my head phones. When I started really dating girls I again found Prince very influential, often speaking on the phone to them in song lyrics. (Ashamed I am) In my personal time I would write erotic Rap songs based on some of my favorite records such as "scandalous" or "Question of U" Eventually a girl would break my heart, my thoughts ranged from killing her, the world. THAT GREEN EYED MUTHA… anyway I had no outlet. I would try to write out my feelings in raps, but I found it binding. Besides you can't get all she broke my heart-ish in a rap record. (Well I wasn't no Drake in my day) So, I wrote my first poem called "Life, Death, Life" I will always remember my first two lines

"WHO WROTE MY LIFE TO BE THIS WAY AND WHY WONT HE LET ME DIE TODAY" I remember this because when my father found the notebook I wrote this in it caused a frenzy in my family, I was forced to see a councilor and the whole deal. From this I learned the power of words. But writing poems would become my daily regimen, to release the pain from what felt like a very stressful teenage life.

When it comes to the artist I ended up becoming, no person has had an impact on me like Tupac Shakur. Just as many young black males of the time related to Tupac. He was a physical representation of the anger, passion, compassion rage and confusion of young black America. His writing was poetic but his delivery was always cryptic (especially his early stuff) I had much compared him to Poe and still do, except Tupac was where I was from and looked like me. The Poetic way he expressed pain is what I clung to most, in fact my pain tattoo is in homage to my favorite Tupac record and my own poetic relationship with pain.

Poetry for many years was just a part of my therapy, when the Def poetry movement started I was like "oh I can't do that" and lived my life.

Poetry was a private conversation I was having with myself. I was always the weird guy over there writing, that was before I stumbled upon a community of weird people writing. People who even considered me a poet, a title I use loosely to define what I do. I was encouraged to open that notebook and share its contents with the world. The response I have gotten on every stage in every city I have ever performed on has been overwhelming. So now, I am humbled and grateful to share myself with you. I titled the book Conversations With Myself because that's how most things I write start. Either I'm asking myself a question or talking myself out of something, the book is divided into five chapters that kind of give you a mind-scope of the man behind the pen. You may not always agree with what you read but I promise you a fun, painful, funny and thought provoking read. You may see sprinkles of Poe, Prince or Pac at any time (maybe even a little Seuss).

I am who I say I am.

I am WrittenInPain.

~~~~~

Chapter One: Follow the Flow…

I thought this would be a good introduction to the book. The very first Poem in the chapter "Twisted Wrist" talks about my conversionary process from thought to pen. This chapter shows the remnant of my M.C. swag in a few pieces. These are the pieces that allow me to exhibit my love for wordplay and rhyme schemes. At times I can hear music when I write so a few pieces actually have a rhythm (in my mind anyway) Sometimes I want to write and not really have an idea of what it is I want to write about. Not a clue. So a few pieces will seem to go places not originally part of the trip…anyway, "Follow the Flow".

Twisted Wrist

It starts with a spark
my hand impatient shaking anticipating the next creation
I dream in rhyme scheme
I compose flows as I doze
my condition pre written position
so my thoughts are yonder
pre ponder...
writing past thoughts... I just caught
head rushed flushed precognition
so the style keeps switching
my pen ink stains to explain my pain
unlocked what I jot flow like locks from the brain
so I'm writteninpain
in two lines
always of two minds
blew mine
when I succumb get numb as a blow line
I borrow inspiration from tomorrow
transcends through my ink pen
sinks in to the depths of what I'm thinking
my muse keeps me confused
no positive support
throughout the visions I sort
closing my eyes not to cry
is how I get lost in thought
no receipt..
for how much bullshit I've bought
hands burned
from all the hell I have caught
sorry...
I tend to get personal in a line or two
how can I see the future but live in the past
cause where I rest

between spirit and flesh
heartless... exhume my chest after my final rest
ask God... or assume the rest
sorry..
I get controversial in a verse or two
hate it or love it
whatever works for you
this is not a poem
these are the sounds my thoughts make ricocheting in my dome
so I pull up rocking chairs at despair's table
most of my brothers were Able's
most of my lovers were not able
to teach me anything but love is a fable..
sorry..
I bring up love sometimes when I rhyme
the topic gets me to crying at the drop of dime
Cupid got some issues
so I shoot first with a bazooka so I won't miss u
lying trying to tell myself I don't miss you
razors to the wrist sounds like bliss
then they think I got issues
sorry...
my pen stride ponders suicide from line to line
I mean time to time
where I sit ... time don't exist
all this
starts from a itch
and a wrist twist

This piece was actually inspired by the Prince song Cream, if you know who he was singing to in that record you will get it.

Loved One

I love you
it wasn't until the day I looked in your eyes
I saw magic
inspiration
dedication and determination
it's a fire in your soul
subdued…controlled
burning still
you are amazement trapped in a person
sexy in essence wrapped in a person
I witness the tormented soul you're searching
I know that you're hurting
yet never ration your passion
you leak talent from your toes
your radiance glows
and..
I love you
I look to you for strength
the words to speak
when life reeks
you are everything to me
if it's wrong to speak to you this way
I apologize
but I get lost in your eyes

I am in awe of you
the moment I saw
the all in you
I confess I'm doing my best to put my all in you
lead me, I shall follow
I want to witness your greatness
some will hate this but
I swear to God… I love you
never again place anything above you
all that will ever matter is you
it's this you you do…
makes you so lovable
your hair
reminds me of power
in the shower run fingers through it for hours
I'm sorry I ignored you
when all along I adored you
even when I felt empty
you never left me
I'm sold
knowing when God made you he broke the mold
I wanna grow old with you
I want to fall in love again
every time you pick up a pen
damn you good..
how do you maintain that blanche of pleasure and pain
no… don't explain
I just want you to know you're motivational
so inspirational
sensational
and I love you…
this bottle of Windex made me see it clearer
and yes mutherfuckers
I wrote this looking in the mirror…

So…Many times in life I have felt like Poetry was my only salvation, my only release from the confines of the hell I was seemed to be trapped in.
In this piece you can see someone actually struggling to maintain sanity. The title was a rip from a Malcolm X speech "The Ballot or the Bullet".

<u>The Poem....or The Bullet</u>

In the asylum of my mind's eye...ramped thoughts escape...
Jumping walls...running through barbed wire...
Exhausted...Dripping Blood they make it out...
Crammed in between parallel lines...
Guided by margins....
If only it was this simple.
See...most times life moves faster than I can write it down....
So it's all post scripted
Not pre-scripted
or pre-dicted
As I hide behind words...
seeming to strip me as they flee from my soul.
Naked I am...
Trying not to lose myself in these tears
Trying to hold my peace
While falling to pieces
For if I have a LOVE…
WORTH LOVING....
Why is it not unveiled to me...
Then why do I only feel the comfort of my shadow...
These are crooked rulers...

Who draw conclusions with crooked rulers...
I've never been Loved!!!
Only serenaded by the lies...lovers tell before they hypnotize you
How can we make Love
If i despise you...
Maybe everyone does ...
I'm just too wise too
Ignorance
is blissfulness
How many times I've been through this
Life's a trip
I got no permission slip
Was u ever my star
or was I just wishing shit..
I don't have the tools to make believe
But I have a pen
Make me breathe
I live through this
EVERY PIECE I EXHALE
frees me
Believe me
Every line is an extension
my painful twisted de-mention
I am not poetry
Poetry is for the free
I am a madman
This is verbal insanity
I play russian roulette with paper mates
Suicidal is my prose
So instead of death
I choose rhyme flows
In the end it's the same
words keep me sane
As they leave the asylum of my brain
witness me go insane....

At the time this was written it was my most personal piece to date. It was the first time I spoke about anything that wasn't emotionally charged. It was an attempt to explain who I was, why I was. This is still one of my favorite pieces because it came from such an honest place; this is/was my life. If you never been to the Bronx, consider this a guided tour. Enjoy.

UR NOT FEELING ME

My skin consists of...
Cement, concrete and steel
Lost within the shadows…
Of living breathing monuments
Like sacred ground I'm bound to it
Them bricks, them streets
Is like my heartbeat
See my soul was born between the 5th floor and pebble beach...
That's project talk for rooftops
Same place we made cherries pop
Hitting Cops with Rocks
as they watched my idols flip rocks for cash knots
Last night they shot Roc
Chased chino out his socks

Same rooftop
Now we letting off glocks
Keeping pigeons by the flocks

My flow was provoked by the fact we was broke
All we had was MC dreams and ganja smoke
Plotting for breadman
Flowing over Redman
We tipped ashes in beer bottles
Them dudes u was afraid to walk pass was our role models
UR NOT FEELING ME
I'm not from NY
NY is in me
I'm from the BRONX
Putting flows to beats was born here
Battle bars birth place, in the first place
Virtues I hold close to me
WHO AM I SUPPOSE TO BE!!!!!
A man is defined by his words
If u not loud u won't be heard
Iron horse gallops overhead
Another neighbor's son is dead
Over bread
I'm from unsubtle rebuttal
Turn gun scuffle
Block party one shot…
Feet shuffle
Home now avoiding piss puddles
This ain't a struggle
It's the everyday hustle
Try to evade the strays and ricochets
My corner was full of dudes looking to get paid a quicker way
UR NOT FEELING ME!!!
We from
Playing tag
To tagging up
packing bags to bagging up
Acting bad to acting up

Night time play in the pool
Now it's night time we playing pool
Rack'em up
One of us caught beef we all had to back 'em up
Street Boppers
Beat Boxers
Slap Boxers
My mind runs along KRS-1
See how the bridge was over before it begun
We label the borough home of the champions
UR NOT FEELING ME !!!!!!!!!
The Bronx birthed lyrical minds
Rooted pride in all our lines
The lyrical capital
We built by design
Bronx finest
Bronx bravest
Bronx legend
LARRY DAVIS
We went from burnt out
To Boogie Down
Timbo's Hooded down
Before Blood's and Crypts came along
It was Spades, Latin Kings and Decepticons
Find the X on the map
That's where the verbal treasures at
Where rhyme flow is measured at
It's just what we better at
Gun fights at Midnight
By morning mural in the lobby
Beer's and candles
His moms trippin' too much to handle
Both her son's were killed to set an example
They were Bronx legends
Babe Ruth. Mickey Mantle
Just because of how they played the game...

Now they gone price of fame
R.I.P beside they name
Moment of silence....
Big Tiny
Black
Remo
Martin Santiago
Nelson Blanco
Mike Moore
Mike was 14 when they put two in his chest
He was only dating a spanish girl
Her brothers kept warning him...
U R NOT FEELING ME !!!!!!!!!
Too many of my tears watered Woodlawn cemetery
Miles Davis is there
I would write poems on his tomb whenever I was feeling Kind of Blue
They took Scott La Rock before Criminal Minded dropped
This is for Tariq and Peter Guns
This is for
Morris Houses
Edenwald
Mott Haven
The Bronx is home
Kiss the pavement
but...U R NOT FEELING ME !!!!!!!!!!!!!!!

Question..#1

Where do poems go to die?
you know,
the ones we forget to write
the lines we forget in the middle of jumbled narratives
or life's sucky distractions
sometimes just know it
till I sit down click my bic
nothing
where is it?
I look, search
maybe it has jumped into another poets mind...
HEY POET GIMMIE BACK MY POEM!!!!!
what about the poems we miss sleeping....
where do they go..
do they go back to that big poem book in the sky
where do poems go to die?

COSMIC RHETORIC

WITH INTROSPECTION
GAIN PERCEPTION
YET RETROSPECTION
REVEALS DECEPTION
REALIZING IN LIFE THERES NO PERFECTION
PAIN IS USED TO OBTAIN CORRECTION
HEARTS LEFT OUT WITHOUT PROTECTION
LOVE AND HONOR NO CONNECTION
ONLY THROUGH TEARS YOU LEARN THIS LESSON
BENDED KNEES WAIT FOR BLESSINGS
AT NIGHT I WHISPER MY CONFESSIONS
MY WRONGS MY LIES, FUTURE
TRANSGRESSIONS
MY LIFE A MAZE OF POINTLESS QUESTIONS
THEN I'm FORCED TO HIDE AGGRESSIONS
DEMONS AT ME WHILE I'm RESTING
WHEN I SMILE I'm ONLY JESTING
FROM ALL THE SHIT I AM DIGESTING
IN THE MIRROR SEE I'm DIGRESSING
IS THIS THE LIFE IN WHICH I WAS DESTINED?????

BODY OF MUSIC

My body is music
My inner thoughts leave my brain with echoes of heavy metal
A screech that can't be broken
I dream moshpits, guitars leaving splinters in my mind
My walk is hip hop find me on the streets
with my stride of beat
My hands have two names Rock & Roll
My eyes are the key board to my soul
By the last key you'll find me
Writing ballots blindly
 My heart the local hangout for memories I can't lose
Like a dim lit club lowly playing the blues
My hair is alternative known by many names
My mouth is Prince, My tongue is Rick James
MY music on sheets
Comes with a Caribbean beat
That's my hips making **you nod**
Between them...oh that's Gospel....making u scream for **God**

Like...

Rainbow flow
Light bends when it transcends
How beautiful the world to the blind man
I write like a madman on his death bed
never knowing which will be my last words
so I scribe about embracing death
'cause dying is cooler when you can convince people
you knew it was coming
I write pieces while I'm typing...
yeah, I said I WRITE pieces while I'm typing
'cause I lose lines while I'm writing
I clinch poems in my teeth
life to me is a sheet of loose leaf
so inside my mind
is introverted rhymes
I combine with dope lines
you hooked?
my pen got you on a syringe binge ?
call me the Scarface of poetry..
Tony Montana in a bandana
say hello to my lil friend
just got high off that YEYO
holding a pen...that was a titanic line.... let that sink in
you know how many words I embezzle
just so I can take poetry to the next level
wasn't focused when I wrote this
this is just a piece
resulting from the peace pipe
puffin' on that bruce banner
sticky as spider-man hands
damn that was pretty... blunt
I'm like Pookie in New Jack I crack myself up
like a drunk whore... I get side tracked
loner

**only my spine got my back
grind hard
so I can quit my day job
but my clock keeps an erection
that mean times hard
dopeman of poetry
so I'mma sprinkle a few lines out**
to leave ya'll strung out like Amy Winehouse
oh too soon...?

I wanted to create a movement, I wanted to tell the world that Poets…that poetry was being overlooked and underappreciated. I wanted to create a battle cry of sorts for the poetic community. I never call myself a poet in the true sense of the word, but understand why I get confused for one... If you notice you will feel a very Hip Hop undertone in this one, however it's the Poetic mantra …at least in my mind.

WE ARE POETS

What's in a word…spoken**?**
in the hands of a word weaver
pretense never intended…
reality not suspended
seamlessly blended
we are not as they are …we use words with precision
viewing the world with Neo's vision
scribing life with a hero's mission
RIP MY HEART OUT MY CHEST PUT IT RIGHT IN A RHYME
We have no filter
We are breathing Quills
Dipping our souls in blood
This is the ink of a poet
truth and light
is this what you think of a poet
we are the raped
the abused
the confused
the molested
the brokenhearted
the outcasted
the black sheep
the adopted
the promiscuous
the poor
the teachers
the reporters
the enlightened
the story tellers
the history keepers
the visionaries
RIP MY HEART OUT MY CHEST PUT IT RIGHT INTO A RHYME

we are poets!!!
we had no choice
no option
the spirit was born in us
light was created from but a word
whats in a word?
once spoken..
the power to inspire thought
we are poets
and although we walk amongst them
we are not as they are
they think about life... on a good day
we..
we are the salt of life
our thoughts are consumed with how to depict life so that the mortals can enjoy its flavor
we are chefs
making alphabet soup
each with a recipe .. irreplaceable
we wilt
but never dying
DONT FEEL PAIN 'CAUSE ITS ALL IN THE MIND
we change our names
we hide our faces
because our hearts are on our sleeve
needing that paper to help us breathe
we are written words in flesh
RIP MY HEART OUT MY CHEST PUT IT RIGHT INTO A RHYME
we are poets

I actually never felt like I wrote this, truth is it was one of those moments that happen when you're creating. That freaky moment when you have lost yourself and all that exists is the Muse. It actually consumed me and when I had finished I was unsure of what happened. I wanted to add this poem because I never want to forget that moment, when my pen took me on a trip.

<u>LOVE LETTER</u>

So, I dip scripts from soul patrols
Astros, past those, from Orion's belt… **make lassos**
black hole near my soul
sucking life from me
no time or space near…
face fear
for fear of reality
for fear being comforted inside insanity
even God can't ha**ndle me**
these scandals dismantle me
part of the devils strategy
lost souls fill vessels
nestled inside zombies
trying to fight the light so the angels can't find me
liquid hell inside of me
speaking in low tones
DEMONS TRY TO QUIET ME
black wings hiding me
St. Peter denying me
body burns
children die violently
crumbled in this concrete jungle
witness the fall of the humble

Armageddon
glad it's here
vengeance for lost souls
vanquished from the stratosphere
in a dark room I was consumed
then cocooned
only the selected will be resurrected
count me among the neglected
I'm infected
sharpened from clay
only born to decay
I CAN HEAR A TRUMPET SOUND
judgement to be passed down
I fear no evil
I fear no flames
I fear no death
call me by name
witness the coming of here after
or then after
neither time nor space
so which overcomes faster
THOU CANNOT SERVE TWO MASTERS
love me or hate me
I am who you make me
follow my open door
it will lead to more
for what do we pursue ?
the very reason we work?
pay our taxes?
go to church?
to feel the misery of a life never living up to its worth?
no....
we desire the freedom to
DO AS THOU WILT
I am only what you make me
and confining your desire will only make you crazy

LUST
would it exist if man was free by his own hand ?
for under the blade of one many have bowed to a command
GREED
is a simple need for more
in fact it is only ambition at its core
for who would keep man from that tree
only he.. who knew more than me
for that he is sworn over me!!!
DANCE
because I can hear the gallops of horses pulling chariots of fire
INDULGE
in your flesh because a darkness shall come before the light
BOW
to your Gods and false idols
I have seen great wonders in the sky
plagues
rumors of war
are these not the days proven far worst then those of Sodom and Gomorra ?
yes.. they are
DO AS THOU WILT
in the distance... I hear a trumpet sound

I AM

I was created in my father's image
Fire...Elo...soul
in my chest faith was invested in me
I create life with words
Let there be light
when I'm on the mic
and it was good..
I was raised with respect
the order of Melchezedic
full of glory head erect
I have tarried in the lustful cities
Miami.. New York
Sodom and Gomorra a fresh
I bowed to no idols
lust for no flesh..(coughs)
and I knew her..
she was no Sarah
so when I tried to proceed
pillar of salt she was indeed
She was Delilah
yet eye
and my locks survived her
Finding shelter in New Jerusalem (more like New Jersey)
even my own people hurt me
am I not worthy
troubled waters got high
I know a way out (Noah way out)
so my green herb was kush
I burned that bush
it spoke to me
when I came down off that peak
had two tablets
one pen

my prophesy begins
so I write to bring awareness to the powers that be
LET MY PEOPLE GO
but their minds are not free
I am like David
if you're around me…I will get you stoned
some compare me to Solomon because he was wise
but he also had 700 wives
so.. I'm really not surprised
I am the son of man
the pen I use
resurrects the dead
and feeds a multitude
find proverbs in my words
just as he spoke against the government
and spoke against the church
that same aim in me
he who can hear will hear
he who sees will see
I love those who believe in me
glad those Judas' that been deceiving me
finally leaving me
surrounded by bodies who are empty
try to tempt me
BARE FALSE WITNESS AGAINST ME
that crown of thorns don't fit me
your arrows fall at my left
fall at my right
none of them hit me
I am the comforter
humph… ask any lady did I comfort her
heavy is the head wearing the crown..
this is true
forgive them father.. they know not what they do

A poet had pissed me off…point blank. The nerve of him right? I know...he thought he was dealing with some prolific motherfucker he ain't know…he ain't know. I use a lot of wordplay in this one, so don't exceed the read limit.

Who?

You be profound
I throw down with pronouns
a spotlight and open mic make you a pro now?
slow down
solidify how the cadence and the flow sound
what I blow
I grow now
so if you need that
you know now
wooow
I'm the shit no constipate
I got the juice no concentrate
It's gonna get crazy so concentrate
flow top shelf
so they book me
plus I roll with a sick dude
I'm one tuff Cookie
dope
like them basements where they cook E
yes I'm addicted to the drug reference
take a crack at it
see if you weed 'em out in a sentence
HOLLOW MAN?
oh 'cause you can't see me
got hollow hands?
back to basics
South Bronx passion my pen is laced with

no
a string of dope lines is what my pens laced with
are you still concentrating with your mind? it would be fishy if you ain't catch them lines
no
its fishy when they get so hooked on the rhyme they bite lines
this ain't a poem
this me getting dirty on a 30-30
30 poems from me?
ya not worthy
YEAH YOU HEARD ME
no
my magic wont assist you
'cause you ain't worthy
too much talking
so we kill little birdies
you know..
all the little tweets that tweet me
a lot of my lines over yawl head like tight ropes
I put heroin in my pen so I write dope
That's my third time using dope in this poem I know
but when you sick.. trying not to be sick it's hard to say
no
I been doing this since seven years old
talk circles round your head
that's just how..I....roll
no
let's cut the mustard
going ham on you turkeys is just how I roll
my verbal display is like sex
I can do this all day
only difference is .. this isn't hard
every line don't make you say "oh my God"
hmm, maybe it do
but at least this.. you'll let your girlfriend read after you

**even though if I jot it
they may read it after you.. and never tell you about it
(wink)**

LOYALTY

Loyalty
you can't find it in the soul of a mother giving her daughter to strange fingers
fingers that have yanked out all honor and respect
Nor is it in the eyes of your lover who secretly plots to love another
It does not rest in the chest of the friend in need using your kindness as a means to beguile you
you will search for it in the ears of those you share your secrets, never knowing that a secret told.. is a secret no more
until your name is as a lyric to a tune
amusing to those who are only loyal to gossip and backstabbing
How long does it take to earn?
For if there was a day…a day that loyalty was the testament of men
it is hidden in crevasses of histories forgotten folklore
Iscariot
Brutus
Cain
we remember these names
Loyalty
broken like the bread you broke with a man
the one on the witness stand
believing lies…telling truths
somebody wanting a body
loyal to their body
a lost cause
like white boys looking for rhythm
lust clouds loyalty
as greed
and jealousy
also envy

as self preservation supersedes them all
many place loyalty in the unfaithful
a foolish investment indeed
Loyalty can only be found in the heart consumed with loves
admiration
loyalty
can only be proportioned …to the loyal
lest we forget this…above all things

This would kinda be a sequel to LOVE LETTER but it was actually me questioning life
maybe I was influenced>> HOPE NOT.

SUBMISSION

Come to me...
why do you hide within the walls of foolish pride
succumb to the grief hollow beliefs bring
why do you mislead yourself?
shun yourself from your ever human desire
liars...all liars
do you really love him more than yourself?
your lives is no reflection of this..
you break trust
bask in lust
full...always craving more
let me flood you with abundance
let me show you the mysterious truth shrouded in darkness
the very universe that surrounds you
the very cloth of creation
darkness
yet I am the brightest star in it
come to me...
purge yourself of any purity you cling to
give in to me
life is for living
not living as a slave ..
free yourself
if your gift is free will
bask in it..
indulge in all of its pleasures
what makes a fruit forbidden
why are truths hidden

because ye are as gods!!
why.. why be confined to everything that strives against your nature
your time in this life too brief for discretion
you body yearns for pleasure
what do the angels in heaven know of pleasure
he commands you not to gorge on the rivers that spring from her fountain
yet her expression seems anything but sinful
you are told not to swallow his staff
yet bow before him willingly
he limits your already limited existence
and why..
is it because of his pronounced jealousy
or is he a dictator...you are nothing more than a pet
come to me...
let me show you the pathway to pleasure unlimited
the depthlessness in true freedoms
do as thy wilt
keep nothing from you
instead let your desires become you
consume you
you were not created to serve
but to live
then live..
with every fiber of your self
why concern your self with what will be after the grave
that will indeed tend to itself
but now while the breath of life be with you
do not be controlled as them before you
do not waste your days hoping
waiting
BELIEVING ...
only fools place hope in what they cannot see
hear
touch

feel...
yet I am here
with you
like I've always been
you are more akin to me then him
why resist..
truth... you have already submitted
come to me
DO AS THY WILT

When I was 21 I got the word PAIN tattooed on my arm, people always asked me why, Tupac was part of the reason. Mainly it was because I had forged a relationship with it. By that age I had discovered that pain is the only constant in life, it has molded me strengthened me and times plagued me. This was my attempt to explain that relationship… pain being universal I'm sure every person will relate to at least one line.

PAIN

Pain
Most fear and avoid it
I embraced it
not to say I enjoy it
I faced it
Only truth I've known
so I relate to it
you hate
I escape through it
we learn lessons from our transgressions
life is only pain at the essence
what don't kill you makes you stronger
we were all bred through tears shed
Pain
remember it as weakness leaving you
when you feel crushed shards of the dreams in you
sometimes you lose yourself being confused
sometimes those are the parts you needed to lose
they ask me how
pains poster child is suppose to smile
my engine is fueled by what's hurts me
naysayers who didn't find me worthy
 conquering the hill I climb

aligned with masterminds
when life driving you crazy you can't see the signs
but when life try to numb you with nonsense
it keeps me conscious
pain
how do you respond to it
I have a religious bond to it
ever laugh so hard it hurt
we scream but live for that thrill
isn't it ironic we all swallow jagged little pills
life hurts in spurts
that's just how it works
we building
so you got to go through the dirt
pain
they say without it nothing's gained
plus it hurts when you go against the grain
pain is the method of my creation
I embrace it with a virgins anticipation
without it who would I be
what would be the content of my poetry
I inhale pain and exhale it poetically
hoping you see the glory in it
I am the beautiful funeral you wish for
my power came from the pain I endured
and I don't bask in it
my gift is my ability to last in it
bites
scratches
slaps across cheeks
oh now pain is good?
hair pulled
some people don't like it
some it gets them excited
pain is a perceived perception
some live life looking for protection

see masochist
and sadist laugh at this
I said pain is a perception
masochist and sadist laugh at this
if it was not necessary
it wouldn't exist
I wrote this for those who use pain to thrive
because pain can make you wish you die
yet the fact we survived
is truly the prize

I was coming into myself with this craft when I wrote this... In truth I was trying to understand myself, how did this thing work? What was the urge to write down feelings, emotions, observations. Why did poets need to get a microphone and share these feelings. By the end of this conversation…I was clear; my hope is you will be as well.

I AM POET HEAR ME ROAR

Visualize what you internalize
intellectualize what you verbalize
what you vocalize I cram between marginal lines
My pens extension for circumvention
what those lost for words find hard to mention
my intention surpass' the grasp of this dimension
life is so full of tension distention
poetry is intervention
from life living
all the turns this life is given
faltered altered decisions so as your living
I make it written
the hope worth hoping for
what written words are spoken for
I am poet hear me roar
I view life in dazes
follow me as I baptize pages
like an apostle speaking gospel
my pen ink the elixir that orchestrate scriptures
causing vibrations
aiding a spiritual congregation
meaning my verbal dispersal is universal
life's motions a circle
my notion is to numb what hurts you
for revealing

that we live through the same feelings
poetry's for healing
frown reversal
life is a stage show
no rehearsal
knowledge pain or entertainment
arriving with what I came with
literal life in metaphor
what written words are spoken for
I am poet hear me roar
notebooks painted tainted
lustfully gained erections
crooked elections
battered women unprotected
battered children undetected
life's wrongs gone uncorrected
ancestral forces I've been selected
ancestral voices resurrected
speaking only what's reflected
pen races across empty spaces to finish lines
the victory is clarity
emotions that you share with me
unity or disparity
wars or senseless casualties
lies and conspiracies
the fear in me
not here with me
fear that you're not hearing me
those that can don't need to
poetry has already freed you
Those that cant have to
if not for self
for those who came after you
just as those before
laid a path for you
what shall be the answer the future ask of you

Let poetry be that open door
what written words are spoken for
I am poet…hear me roar
for paying homage to those who founded you
the celestial forces surrounding you
the light of love found in you
to those energies first born son pregnancies
the continuation of legacies
secret recipes
home grown remedies
powers from Psalm singing
fighting invisible enemies
thunder claps
rain dance in a drummers circle
when lighting speaks
the village listens
like ears being christened
forged in truth
myth becomes legend
legend becomes mere folklore
never forgetting those who came before
what written words are spoken for
I am poet…hear me roar

FOLLOW THE FLOW

follow the flow
if I tell you to follow me
I don't claim to be king
I just know putting the number one
in front of zeros
is the only way it will amount to anything
I'm pet spray
ticked off
Cobb county
big boss
congratulating the overrated
Rick Ross
ya'll ass backwards
Kris Kross
flight oceanic
get lost?
follow the flow
you think you hot
I'm an A.C
told you from the Genesis
I'm not a Gameboy
so don't try to play me
you better than me
that's a dreamcast
mad at me
cause wii
hit the same ass
so don't blame me
while you're on your Playstation 3
I'm hitting your ex-box
follow the flow
I spit hot fire
like a demon screaming
you spit like a chick

scared of semen
call me captain dick
I keep chicks full of sea-men
and if loose lips sink ships
I got titanic dick
if you in shape
get fucked out your fit
pound it
till you mimic porn star sound clips
follow the flow
they used to call me baking soda
I was always armed with hammers
till I seen wrestling with that
only leaves bodies in slammers
see where I'm from
you're either on the court
shooting the rock
or in court cause you shooting over rocks
I chose bars better served for life sentences
call my pen-a-tentiary
to paper mates I make do a bid with me
follow the flow
let me let down my hair then
cause when I come off the head
my trigger is hairpin
so racing me to finish lines
really isn't fair then
never rushing when I gun by
ya'll pen be blushing
you gun-shy
follow the flow
high as a satellite when I write
my pen is polite
that means I'm nice
and if its murder she wrote
it's genocide when I scribe

I lay em' down
futon
leave them crumbled
crouton
bout to bury him
put a suit on
better than me?
cut it out...coupons
you don't want to meet defeat
keep your shoes on
follow the flow
no need for a hand
I'm a man myself
that's why I'm in such demand myself
no need for labels
I brand myself
so hot
gotta fan myself
legs keep breaking
I can't stand myself
I'm a wolf
just know how to pull the wool over myself
make room in my belly to eat poets
I'm so full of myself
follow the flow
want my pen scribe it then
want my life survive it then
speak to the demons that lie within
coming in for a landing
I'm high again
allow me to reintroduce myself
hi again
against me
bad luck I keep penicillin on my dick
I'm a sick fuck
follow the flow

follow the flow like perky tits
or Dorothy on roads made of yellow bricks
I aspire to inspire
that's what I do this for
raise a bar
hope people won't accept garbage anymore
once your labeled garbage you stuck with it
I have a chastity belt on my pen
so you can't fuck with it
I got a midas pen
don't suggest you try this pen
better than me?
wrong again
writing a weak poem reminds me of my dick
that's how loooong its been
follow the flow

Chapter Two: The re-education of WrittenInPain

Life is about growth; my belief is someone should make it a duty to learn something new every day. I often ponder what things people thought about before the world became overwhelmed with distractions. As a society it seems we have been trained not to think for ourselves, instead we have become a sheeple, easy accepting of what we are told to think. In a world filled with projected perceptions it's easy to become mislead…misinformed. As creative writers, poets especially, there is an obligation to inform. The inception of Hip Hop was not about rich people making songs about how rich they were pretending to be. It was a voice from the underdogs, the voiceless and they had a lot to say. I grew up listening to Public Enemy, Krs-One X-clan the list goes on. I titled this chapter "The Re-education of Writteninpain" because as you learn things you are forced to unlearn things. In my adult life I have been able to disprove most things I learned about history in elementary school. I think about the masses who haven't, this goes onto most things we are programmed to accept. Even the Bible.

This collection of writings is not intended to offend anyone's personal religious or political views. Just a singular perception from the voice of the underdog. I don't intend or expect you to agree with it all, however maybe…maybe it can cause you to ask a question about something you thought you knew. Maybe it will encourage you to reeducate yourself. Please read this chapter with an open mind. I promise you will be different when it's done.

FUTURE IMPERFECT

FROM WHERE I'm STANDING I SEE A GENERATION
OF CHILDREN PLUGGED INTO DEVICES FROM
THEIR POCKETS FROM THEY WRIST WATCHES
FORCE FED INFORMATION
FROM UNSUPPORTED SOURCES...CAUSING
VIRUSES IN THEY MINDS
I SEE BOOKS LOOKED UPON AS ANCIENT RELICS
FROM AN AGE WHEN MAN THOUGHT FOR
HIMSELF
WHEN HE COULD THINK FOR HIMSELF
WHEN HE COULD THINK...PERIOD
I SEE BLACK MEN BONDED CHAIN GANG STYLE
BEING HAULED OFF INTO PACKED
CONCENTRATION CAMPS....OH I MEAN
PLANTATIONS...I'm SORRY...PENITENTIARIES
THOSE THAT WERENT WERE REDUCED TO
INDENTURED SERVITUDE...SORRY I MEAN
MINIMUM WAGE LABOR
I SEE A SCHOOL SYSTEM SHREDDED REDUCED
TO INATTENTIVE DAYCARE
BUILDING UR MIND TO STAY THERE
BREEDING ANYTHING BUT SCHOLARS
THEIFS KILLERS HUSTLING FOR INVISIBLE
DOLLARS
A SLANT IN DIVISIONAL POWER
SO WE ARE REDUCED TO TOOLS
PAWNS FOR POLITICAL FOOLS
DRAIN MONEY OUT OF SCHOOLS
TO SPEND, KILLING, DRILLING, SPILLING FOSSIL
FULES
BABIES ARE PUSHING STROLLERS
I'm CONFUSED.....

REALIZING I WAS LOOKING TOO FAR INTO THE FUTURE...IMPERFECT
SO I'm BACK TO NOW...FELLING LIKE EBENEZER AFTER THE THIRD GHOST
I RAN DOWN THE BLOCK SCREAMING
SNATCHING HEAD PHONES OUTTA CELL PHONES
TELLING EVERY ONE WHO WOULD LISTEN
"Think about the future!"
THEY LOOKED AT ME.....NON BELIEVERS
BELIEVING I WAS A ZEALOT, OR SOME MAD MAN ACTING MAD.....I WAS
MAD MY NEPHEW WAS IN THE 5TH GRADE AND COULDN'T READ
MAD CAUSE, WHAT GOOD IS EDUCATION
TO A TRIBE LOST OF INSPIRATION
THERE'S A LINE BEING DRAWN
BETWEEN THOSE THAT HAVE
AND THE NEVER GONNA' GETS
CHILDREN RARLEY PLAY ANYMORE
HOW YOU GOING TO GET THEM TO LEARN
Think about the future
THERE IS A BOY SOMEWHERE
P.S. ANYWHERE
DREAMING HE WAS
LIL WAYNE
DWAYNE WADE
'CAUSE DOCTORS AND LAWYERS ...DONT GET MAGAZINE COVERS
THIS MACHINE WE LIVE IN
DILUTING FREE THOUGHTS
CREATING DRONES
MINDLESS CLONES
PLUGGED INTO DEVICES WITH HEAD PHONES
BOPPING TO IGNORANCE
LISTENING TO A FELLOW HIGH SCHOOL DROPOUT

BELIEVING HE GONNA' MAKE IT
SHOUT OUT TO LEBRON...BUT
KIDS NEED TO KNOW...THEY WORTH MORE THAN GAMES
HOLLOWED GOLD CHAINS
WHAT FEEDS THE EYES KILLS THE BRAIN
Think about the future
OVER 100 YEARS SINCE DOUGLAS TAUGHT HIMSELF TO READ
WE'LL NEVER REPLACE MALCOLM OR MARTIN...
SHIT I'D SETTLE FOR A 2PAC
I'm STANDING IN NOW
ONLY BOOK THEY READING
SAY FACE ON IT...(wink)
GUSHY BRAIN MOUSE CLICKERS
JOGGING SLOW ON THE INFORMATION HIGHWAY
IN 5 YEARS WILL BE MOURNING INTELLECT
CONSCIOUS REASONING WILL BE WHAT OLD FOLKS TALK ABOUT...
I HOPE THE SPIRITS OF THOSE WHO FIRST INTEGRATED SCHOOLS WILL FORGIVE OUR FAILURE
I SEE THE FATE FROM HERE
IT'S A FUTURE IMPERFECT
    PLEASE
    PLEASE
Think about the future

I was actually listening to the good Dr. Phil Valentine when the seed for this piece was planted. You ever seen pictures of Mars surface? There are structures on it that closely resemble pyramids and sculptures own in Kemet. Well when I first saw them it sent me and my pen on a rocket ship time machine. When I got as far back into the past as I could get…I slowly crept forward. This piece was the end result.

HUE R U?

So after the cooling of Mother Earth
When her Tempest Magnus had settled
When the bombardment of galactic particles succeeded in swaying her emotions
There was peace!!!!!
The darkness which nestled her,
 illuminated with celestial wonders,
and moving pieces of infinite wisdom all…designed by the very breathing….ever moving….ever creating….
on this night
for your benefit of understanding….
I SHALL CALL …..G O D !!!!!!
Such a small word, when you begin to digest just how vast infinity is outside the limits of blue skies u bow 2
The realization of conscious energy limitless destinations…
It flows in a cypher, of circulation….
Returning to its source
This is the spirit of life
Inside this living entity called earth…CONSCIOUSNESS
Realization of the self…and its relationship to all things….
Is the comet conscious of itself

As it moves through the galaxy
Only to return
This is life's cycles
360 degrees
See
Energy is never destroyed…
Only deployed
It finds itself forming in the dust of the mother continent
For it is written…wind was blown into my nostrils and I inhaled the very breath of my spirit
For am I not one with she
Water consumes her body
and at her center…hot liquid breathing creation
at its core
Am I not the same
For if I am framed of earth
Is my body not consumed with water?…
Do I not breathe the same air as she does?…
The Darkness which is the knowledge of the very fabric of the universe
Is this not my skin
At my core, does not a fire burn within?
How can I maintain 98 degrees?
Unless I am a star
Meaning all life here orbits around me
It's useless to disagree
I was constructed from everlasting
For eternity
Meaning the universe
Is inside of me
Spiritual minds
Move consciously
Through consciousness
For sake of argument
call it righteousness
For it is written

The spirit moves through the wind
Hovering over waters collection information
That matriculate through our bodies
So from the earth
Near flowing waters
The Nile
Euphates
The Tigris
Creation was formed
Civilization was born
Where were u?
U were doubts attempt at self purging
Just as when sickness, enters the body
Before it corrupts the entire body
White blood cells are replicated
Then banished
You are perfection Imperfection
Lower level species
Fasting on death
Feasting on death and feces
Hiding in caves because u feared nature...and yourself
As u counted toes
Pyramids were erected to pay homage
to the energy that has cultivated us mind, body. and
spirit that at this hour for your sake of overstanding
WE SHALL CALL......GOD
A word birthed on a foreign tongue...
To limit that which is limitless
We are children of universal order...splendiferous.
Planetary Parents
to those adorned with color it was apparent
For when he still believed the world was flat
We had already charted maps
If the sun is round...
The moon is round
Higher consciousness will handle that

Before the wind was at his back
We had cultivated the world and came back
In fact it was residual intellect that even allowed you to crawl from your ice cold …prison
You saw, Sun children, the universe's selected….
In skins of Bronze and Gold
Did not the ancient Mexicans bow to Quetzalcoatl
As did the Yellowman
              Redman
               Sandman
Before you invented telescope to see
We scripted secrets of astrology
For it is written,
Check the stars for signs and a child will be born
This hate goes deeper than complexion
Or natural selection
Ask the Native Americans
For as the sun shines…and the earth turns
It is only u that burns
U hate nature
So for your leisure
U wreck creation…
U don't create
U decl'mate
Desecrate
Nature Hater
Death creator
You took the earth
sucked her dry
erased the past…
blackened the sky
Coated her with cement
fed her lies
It's the melanin
Conductor of rhythmic tones
U cast destruction from your bones

U r every fraction
A reaction
To natural actions
U are death in flesh
Lord of cannibalism...
Lust and incest
See earth children were harmonious
Before your inception
Before your laws of lies and deception
Atom bombs, deathly weapons
U searched the glob for your history
yet everywhere u turned...there was me
U r revenge was to re cultivate me
Bind me spiritually
To a European mindset that cause me to accept your
damnation ...as I wait patient ...for a redemption...
from a source that for the sake of your own
innerstanding
I .....WILL...CALL.....G O D !!!!!!!
How can 3000 years of your lies
supersede 2.5 million years of spirituality
How can cave dwellers teach the universal order
To those who adorn cosmic flesh
As we unravel times illusion
Karmic energy will find a solution
It is from darkness....where light is born
I know who I am....
HUE R U?

I was talking with some teenagers about the Bible. They were with some kind of church leader in the park. He made reference to us, meaning Afro-Americans being more fortunate then our African brothers and sisters on the mother continent. When I asked him how so exactly I assumed he was going to tell me about us having food, clean water, etc. But what he said actually changed my life forever; he said we were more fortunate because we got to know Jesus. This only perplexed me because we got to know Jesus through slavery. The world got to know Jesus through bloodshed. So because I needed clarity from this man of the church I wanted to make clear what he said. I asked him "are you saying God let our ancestors go through 500 years of rape, murder, lynching, degradation and mental destruction that of which we still have not recovered from… so that same man could show us Jesus". He said yes, and judge not the messenger. However you receive that, I have no opinion. What I will share with you is my opinion.

KAMIKAZE

Check out the subtext or dissect my dialect
Minuscule insects swatted by intellect
Inject self respect into your cerebral cortex
Or get snapped, trapped in a verbal vortex
Who Am I?
The opener of eyes
Revealer of iconic lies
Where history lies
Wisdom's words never wasted on the wise
Religion is division
See it

Third eye vision
Between divination and translation
The truth got missin'
But the proof not missin'
Those scared of the light might not listen
Religion was created to control the masses
Gods were created to put fear in their asses
Myth becomes legend
When enough time passes
Legends become lies
The truth burns to ashes
Churches become cash stashes
Religion is big business
CAN I GET A WITNESS?
Followers need leaders
Lies need believers
A nation founded by crooks
Yet...
You don't investigate who gave you the books
Taught you to pray and who to obey
Could it be true?
He without spirit
Spiritually cultivated you
Are we to rejoice at slavery
Because he who enslaved brought Jesus to me
What became of the Gods of my ancestry
Let's get this right....
I reject my God
Because through slavery
This white man saved me
So after the whipping and the raping
Served the God...
That HE gave me
If that don't sound crazy
Catholics tell us Virgins are having babies
How can you gain logic

From the homo-erotic
Meek, Sweet, Turn the other cheek
He doesn't even follow the words that he speaks
Everything he told you
Part of the system built to control you
Waiting for a new age prophet
Not for profit
All I see is preachers in pimp outfits
Begin your mental transformation
Free your mind from the Plantation
Fight fear
Evoke a spiritual emancipation
Joshua to Jesus
Illogical translation
Joshua means the way to the light
Jesus means HEY ZEUS
Something isn't write
Some may see this as blasphemous
Yet...Can't understand why they laugh at us
They netted, sold, bought and branded us
Yet...We bow to the God they handed us
They netted, sold, bought and branded us
Yet...We bow to the God they handed us
They netted, sold, bought and branded us
Yet...We bow to the God they handed us
FREE YOUR MIND!!!!

Striptease

Some bow knees not knowing who they pray to
a father with a mass of children that don't obey u
so they chant down the devil in Lucifer's tongue
they toss stones in glass houses when they live in one
they pray for forgiveness
but won't give you none
Egyptians prayed to the sun...

in return built a great civilization
so why God won't give US one
that's right
suffer in this life
walk the path of the Nazerite
I wonder
how many Bible thumpers
even read numbers
only place it teaches
how to be holy wholly
never hear this from the preachers
they just want you to hear the Jesus piece
be meek...turn the other cheek
isn't THIS the nation indivisible under God
then why do God's people get it so hard...
oh yeah...we blame that on the devil
the fork tongue liar
who spews the same lies as the priest and the choir
with they pedophiliac desires
oh they demons too
but don't they kneel to the same God as you?
I'm confused
but you'll quote Psalms for an excuse
hey wait...
how did us and Jesus get introduced?
oh people died...
dragged...hog tied
death and toucher to all who denied
books were burned
I would go further but you're not concerned
u gonna say I got the devil in me
so
let me thank the slave master now
for erasing my spirit
and giving me a new one
better than the sun

one who watches babies get stomped
and men get hung
one who watched a nation be ruled by his enemies
this goes on for centuries
I kno ...
wait...the kingdom is coming
the heathen shall scatter
wicked start running
all this suffering... this God is perfect
and the 500 years of oppression makes it all worth it
babies in Africa starving
I guess they deserve it
so...I guess we can keep blaming the devil
whoever that is
since he always busy...
and it seems God never is.....

WHERE IS GOD?

does he live in the clouds…sitting on a **throne surrounded by harp players?
does God talk like a Viking?
and what is there to do in heaven…FOREVER??
did you think about that…?
how much you love your car
your flat screen TV
your house… the NBA???
I'm saying, cause none of the shit you like is there…
pizza
hot dogs
sex…
spirits don't have sex and since God sees all things
how horny will you get in the house of the Lord
I'm asking because I often see people attached to** things that I know ain't in heaven yet if I ask them they will say that'**s where they wanna go when they die confusing indeed…**
most people scared to die…
**yet dying is the only way u get to heaven..
so why do people cry so much when people die?…aren't they going to a better place…**
anyplace I can't watch basketball….is not **better but that is my opinion…
anyway are u crying cause u gonna miss them? well** that's selfish … it's almost like your hating I mean they **are going to a better place…right?
and about seeing them again…well the Bible said we** won't notice our love**d ones all we will see is God…**
hmmmm so the people you have lost you won't see **them again ….heaven sound a lil over rated…**
now back to God…is that why we were made to suffer **in a life just so that when we die we can be bored to** death…?

'cause heaven **sound like church…and church is boring**…AS HELL
(no pun intended)
 now don't get it twisted hell don't sound like it's all that **much fun either… but I understand that if your evil or a bad person going to a place where you will be made to suffer forever by your ever loving all merciful forgiving father who made you and loves you…**
but if I'm good and live clean all I have to look forward to is clouds and harps and more serving my father… this sounds familiar
I wonder if that's clouds in heaven or is **that cotton… listen I'm changing my heaven…**
first of all my God talks like Ozzie Davis …shit looks like him too
and it's no clouds… **its benches and stoops and cars to sit on…**
how imma be dead someplace with James Brown
Michael Jackson
The Temptations
Four Tops
2Pac
Biggie
Big Pun
Tito Puente
Jim Morrison
Jimmy Hendrix
Bob Marley
and all we gonna hear is harps …yeah right we jamming… all our grandmammas and great grandmammas cooking mac and cheese hush puppies and greens everyday all day….
now I won't mind if the sisters wear them lil loin cloths..

we don't have to listen to Moses, Jesus and God with
that thou, art, thus those crap... we got Martin, Malcolm, W.E.B. Dubois like we got mofos that can talk deep shit..
anyway if you want me to be good u better tell me heaven some shit like that ...
'cause ummmm yeah
where's God at?

Did you know psychologist created the television? I didn't either, ever think about why? Me either, just watched it. Yet this thing is in everybody's home, some homes every room. Everybody watches it …you spend more time with it then anything else. Make you think, what if the people who were in charge of what came on it had wicked intention? What if it was really designed to brainwash you, make you want to buy things. Tell your children how to think…dress…dance. I mean this thing is in your house, it's like a member of the family…You trust it don't you? I mean you leave your kids alone with it? I stole the title from my late Uncle Kenny who always called it that.

TELL- A-LIE-IN-VISION

Something in my home is a cloaked enemy
consciously blocking me spiritually
a enemy who attacks subliminally
a portal to a demonic realm unleashing spirits into my dwelling
infiltrating my mind with lyrics, chimes and subconscious designs
eyes open to the blind
are you not suspicious
saturated content vampires and witches
I was raised Vampires and Witches were bad
so it appears
what was once feared
now cheered and revered
brain faster than the eye
hey, what was that just went by?
What's the deal with the baby on family guy?
conscious queens replaced
with whores showing their behind

IS RIHANNA DOING DEVIL SIGNS?
What's with all the hand gestures?
what do they really mean?
easier to hide things in plain sight
so they are never seen
NIKE was a God of war
what u think his swoosh is for?
isn't it the apparel every great athlete wore?
lighting is the sign of the devil
also the mark of Thor
so what do you think Gatorade put it on the bottle for?
How can you support a war not clear on what they fighting for
is anyone attacking U.S soil?
is it about religion?
or about some oil?
we won't know cause the media is paid off
so let's see who won the american idol
who's in the NBA playoffs
you have no clue what bills were signed
but you know who has a fake behind
you can't point out your appointed senator
but if that ain't the shame...
you know all your favorite celebrity babies names
you don't question where the chem-trails fall
but you question if Beyonce was ever pregnant at all
SEX IN THE CITY
DESPERATE HOUSE WIVES
this isn't fiction it's the days of our lives
reality TV
yet TV scripts the real in reality
alternate versions of beauty
fake nose
fake lips
fake hair
fake hips

make up
fake finger tips
PERFECT
corporations own the news
that's how we know what political parties get defeated
instead of knowing how the cows you eat get treated
like the words of a séance commercials get repeated
like the words of a séance commercials get repeated
like the words of a séance commercials get repeated
like the words of a séance commercials get repeated
until your convinced that you need it
eyes open?
still can't see it?
just another channel
channeling what?
just another station continue your ride
IS THE CBS EYE WATCHING YOU
that box you got turned real... igital
time delay replay... delete... re edit what he say
could you tell?
the real reason them towers fell?
look at this broad
she just won a grammy award
thanking the Lord?
do all whores go to heaven?
depicted as half naked?
televised lies
white writers
black lives
teach your children little white lies
IN 1492 COLUMBUS SAIL THE OCEAN BLUE
I question if that shit is even true
the original maps
charted by blacks
someone changed the facts
we never thought the world was flat

HOW ABOUT TV TALK ABOUT THAT!!!!
or what that Kanye song in reverse say
skull and bones
the boule
they pic your heroes
choose your villains
infiltrate your home
brainwash your children
you'd never even know
how they have been affected after watching that show
the TV is in their room doors close
violating your child right under your nose
we won't talk about how that network
I SAID WE WONT TALK ABOUT HOW THAT NET......
WORK
something in my home is a cloaked enemy
consciously blocking me spiritually
so I tune into the light
praying...it deliver me

My Dad would always use the word "Tricknology". When I was young I didn't understand it. He would say "You like Rocky movies 'cause you don't see the Tricknology behind it". I still like Rocky movies… but I do see the Tricknology behind it. I look for the Tricknology behind all things, that's where this piece came from why didn't I call it Tricknology… beats me.

Questions

Who invented Television…**and why?**
Columbus discovering America … why feed us that lie?
What's a straw man?
Why does he have my name?
Is God and country one in the same?
Do rappers hate women?
Why do they wear a crucifix…? while singing about sinning
Are we safe?
What's with the cameras all over the place?
Can something already inhabited be discovered?
Is America at war with people of color?
At home and overseas?
Raping and plundering once abundant countries?
Why don't they tell the truth on the news?
Is this a war over fossil fuels…
Did I say something wrong?
Why do women dance to misogynist songs?
How many Iphones will black people buy?
I'm speaking to the ones struggling to get by
Why is it so hard to see?
Apple ain't gonna place one cent in your community
Oh you don't care?

It's funny...every nigga got a apple product
Wonder how many work there
You lying
Ain't nothing but Mexicans on those assembly lines
What's a Black College?
Or a urban poet? R&B music? This place is
racist...don't act like you don't know it.
How come the fast track to a black actor's success...is
having a half breed baby...and wearing a dress?
What happen to all the "White Americans" in the NBA
Are we headed towards a future where everyone's
gay?
Homophobia... and pro life ...I make a distinction
if we all turn gay... wont that lead to extinction?
Why is MSG in everything you eat and drink?
someone is poisoning ya mind you think?
course not
Picture McDonalds getting a boycott
How come fast food cheaper than real food?
While healthy food not even in your budget
Is someone trying to keep us sick?
not being negative about the country you love
but the country you love..
loooooves to sell drugs
selling unhealthy food...why would they stop it?
when selling drugs to the sick turns over one hell of a
profit
What is cancer?
What is Aids?
Do you think we getting played?
Don't Magic Johnson look good?
Who decided to make guns black?
Can you answer that?
Oh right...it don't matter?
why are tennis balls green?

Why do sisters always show their ass in these magazines?
You want to be respected for your mind?
yet it's all designed to enhance the behind
Do y'all mind...?
Dudes just spontaneously dancing from behind?
Who made the skinny jeans sag a fad?
What do your kids watch?
Do you even know?
How much subliminal messages attacked them that show?
After school do you teach them anything they REALLY need to know?
Oh you trust in the teacher...?
As well as the Preacher?
OOOOOH YOU ONE OF THOSE EAT WHAT EVER THEY FEED YA?
Bullshit on the menu
they never asked you to try it
I wonder if they sold you KNOWLEDGE would you buy it
do you know the plan?
shorting your life/attention span
to control Africa..
IRAN IRAQ PAKISTAN
was I suppose to say that?
Bill Gates just made another 25 million homeless
people sleeping in abandon buildings
Does that make sense?
Why is the richest country in the world pretending to be poor?
Or is the fact that it's poor motivating the war?
Cause who really uses paper money anymore?
education has diminished to shit
that's why I made this piece long
so dummies won't finish it

did I offend you?
see the erosion of the mind?
how that depleted attention got you skimming lines?
It's not cute
why would you give a child fruit flavored candy instead
of the fruit?
What's the reason for the metal alloys you digest?
who trained you to eat peaches from the can?
instead of fruit when its fresh?
have YOU ever cut peeled and ate a pineapple?
yeah that's a stretch.
Ok but that pink salmon in a can is good?
see that was a test
how come the fish in the can cost less?
but its worst on the body when it's time to digest
oh snap...DE-GEST
DIE-IT
death and food co related?
Let's keep that quiet
did you know that your dentist and the FDA run in the
same crew?
That's why things that rot your teeth get FDA approved
so they can gain a lot of cash
plus you got spare teeth to lose
Why do they tell you condoms are HIV prevention?
oops one of those things I wasn't suppose to mention?
how come so many African American males crowd
these state detentions ?
when in these states the black man is the lowest
demographic
I say them some white washed mathematics
like a black man
do most crimes
most times
most of the time
is that true?

or is that all FOX news will report to you?
Tyler Perry and Oprah got a billion for two
"what, cause I'm black and you black mean I got to do shit for you"
not at all..
plus we dummies
so buy black ain't how we invest our money
it's a funny ride
ya'll niggas let Obama slide
YAAAAY black president I'm just here for the ride.
Did you forget that he lied?
oh I'm not bashing, some of my best friends are liars
all I'm saying is when he finishes this dance
when the "NEXT" president comes
do you think you have a chance..?
I meant do you believe our beef will be legit?
he gonna say…you had 8 years of Obama and ya'll ain't make him do shit?
did I get off topic?
What's milk chocolate?
they love to slip soy on you the best
Do you wonder why men are growing breast?
no? oh?
pumping men full of estrogen
why are there so many lesbians..?
ohh wasn't suppose to say that again?
but it's the chain effect I expect
if men not men anymore
what do women need them for?
well…answer this for me please
why is the South riddled with STD's?
Why do black women lead the globe in aborted pregnancies?
How come they only adopt black children from overseas?
I know why…but I won't discuss conspiracies

so in conclusion...the sum of today's lesson
you need to always know the answer
cause they bound to change the question.

Ok...I was on YouTube and I saw this guy show that it was three 6's embedded in the Disney logo. True it was a shared perception; however it did get me to thinking...in this place we live, nothing is as it seems. Almost like everything is a scheme...cloaking a nightmare calling it a dream!!! Ooops, got carried away.

PLAIN SIGHT

open mouths don't see well
conscious nonsense snubs the subconscious
artificial knowledge
public school wont prepare you for college
maybe? city or community
GED never see a university
sounds like a planned scam to me
a system that produces criminals and mid level workers like a factory
most kids drop out by tenth grade is what they say
they would know... the system is created that way
how can a nation of mediocre education...
be delegated as an authority on how to be educated
another trick for the mind?
is this the same nation that leads the world in crime?
Globally menacing
modeling citizens
packing prisons for that free labor waver
as youths they plant the ability to believe lies in your memory
Santa...tooth fairy...oh white supremacy
General George Washington the brave...killing his black babies...and fucking slaves
I keep thinking 'bout those three 6's in that Disney logo
and how that thanksgiving story was a bullshit promo...
and Ernie and Bert were really...never mind

but when seeds get planted...consider the farmer
if the war is against the mind...who gave you that armor
that history book...who was the author
from who's perception do we learn these lessons
it's not the professors profession to answer your questions
he will...only as it pertains to testing
33rd degrees
Ivy leagues
segregation in education
takes dollars to be a scholar
it's a set up ..
your brain can detect it
that's why as a child initially you reject it
you get broken down...
train to memorize what's written down
those who can't be trained get sighted as difficult
re-evaluated
charted...labeled...then medicated
"YOU G on' LEARN TODAY"
learn how to earn the American way
school is job training
not brain training
how much are these kids retaining
high school is how they shift and sort 'em out
get them sold on the bullshit
or into computers
the rest go to jail.. get pregnant
or talk to recruiters
why you think it's so few that get through
school only teaches you how to be taught what to do
the money college burns
only for a paper that says you can earn
more than you would have without it
but that extra money you spend going where
so who really made the profit?

do people go to institutions to learn more or earn more
cause that's not the same thing
I can show you how to operate or build a plane
is that one in the same?
like you can have a nice apartment
die before you own your home
I can teach you to use
but not build a phone
you can work for my corporation
but never have your own..
some people will say that I'm talking straight ignorance
maybe so...
but I bet your educated ass ain't see them three 6's
in that Disney logo

Remember The Children

who remembers the children
to ask this is to unmask this problem
they don't use pencils
just pushed through institutions
without the essentials
that's why my people losing the human race
can you be a lawyer or doctor with tats on your face
pants below the waist
what a waste
easy catch for the chase
catch another case
school is prison preparation
learn to live in incarceration
they make you memorize lies
crammed program
everybody's body embodies a toxin
what's in these pills they popping
who remembers the children
the gimmicks and tricks in politics
currency and global order
has nothing to do with your sons and daughters
who feeds them chemically altered beef
candies that rot the teeth
are they reading
books
really.. have you seen one
a book?
or a child with one
telephones and toy guns
being a soldier was fun
until he becomes one
who's gonna write the poetry?
who remembers the children
starving in basements of tenement buildings

momma chose drugs over hugs
wondering if hunger feels like love
thrusting for affection
a fathers protection
its helpless feeling hopeless
the future is bleak itself
if it can't speak for itself
who remembers the children

Diary Of The Unwanted

first there was love
wasn't it?
had to be
followed by a heartbeat
beating
beating
this is the music making me
living before becoming conscious
yet conscious I am living
growing
breathing..
I can hear her...
she is the base line to my sound track
growing still knowing
one day my eyes will be all she cares for
this is love isn't it?
her life is my life's livings
engulfed in her core
knowing there is more
as I perform summersaults to remind her
I am anxious to live in that world
the one she lives in full of the sound
creating the music I dream to
I WANT TO LIVE
how long will it take before I can verbalize this desire
will I even remember this place
this time
when I could feel her
loving me...this, is love isn't it?
holding stead fast to dreams
this life a lullaby
SHAKING
HEART BEAT DOUBLES

Something's wrong with her
I can feel her pain
as I feel the pain
like a hot rod piercing my leg..
through my thigh
another through my head
out my eye
why???
another
another
then...
silence
this feeling overcoming me
numbing me
feeling nothing like the oasis of life
she feels cold to me
distant
I am literally melting away
it ..it doesn't hurt anymore
but this is not peace
this is not love
Is it?
heartbeat
beating
beating
beating
then...
music stops....
(please ladies stop having sex without love)

Sometimes we all get a bad rap…Let me finish, let me finish. Sometimes we all get a bad rap. If you wasn't there, it all becomes hearsay. This piece is not about the Devil
or any kind of satanic agenda. *It's more about perception mixed with assumption and how influence can change both. I can't tell you how much of what we think we know is based on things we didn't learn simply told. And yes...in life sometimes we all get a bad rap.*

LUCIFER

How profound
lighting starts from the ground
matter heating matter creates that sound
held in his hand
Holy am I?
for when they reached the frame of perfection
death was Imminent
anything completed can't grow
so…
I awakened them
showed them ignorance was a lie
that higher creation was in the minds eye
evil am I?
in who's eyes
I am the brighter morning star
meaning the sun
truth to my story
I was made framed in the Image of his glory
Can you understand the plan was mandatory
so then I am the serpent?

yet the ancients placed the serpents on their head dress
was it to be unblessed?
but they had the greatest civilization ever established
Did Abraham not come from the land of serpents?
isn't it true?
turning a rod into a snake the first thing God empowered Moses to do?
is it still used today?
is the field of medicine demonic to you?
but it saves lives
my name means one who brings light
bringing light is evil?
is that right?
who told you that?
who showed you that?
oh is it that telephone game?
convincing you a serpent, a dragon and me
one in the same
I bet
yet
my name is Lucifer
not Bahphomet
who claimed I was evil
when did I deceive you
listen
even Job was done with God's permission
even tempting Jesus was only a test
to assure he was blessed
but even in both of those it was Satan you see
and who even told YOU
Satan was me?
my name is Lucifer
meaning he who bares light
a devil is anyone who lived backwards
someone with no cultural pride

capable of murder and genocide
one who operates against natures functions
who's whole mentality is built for distraction
sun burning his skin a natural reaction
rapes plunders enslaves
cloaks it as being brave
covers truth with lies to disguise what he did
poison your babies and brain washes your kids
he diluted your image of Jesus
tricks you into killing your fetus
collectively stimulates you sexuality
lies to you
so you don't know god actually resides in you
he raises a demonic nation
sprays the sky
controls the population
a person with that much negative destructive energy
well… that's the devil to me
it's a game to me
he enslaved your ancestry
makes TV places pictures in that frame you see
to make you love him
and blame it all on me
Lucifer
if it wasn't for me
if she
ain't eat off that tree
could you believe
right now it would still be
just Adam and Eve
no you
nor none of the things you love to do
some people won't like this poem
truthful as it is
it's funny how you let the devil..
tell you…who the devil is

my name is Lucifer
and I was made in the image of my father

If Jesus was With Us

I was riding the train south bound the other day when this brother got on.
He was wearing this huge gold chain
guess it was gold
hanging from it was this large crucifix…
Guess that was supposed to be gold too
it had Jesus on it…
Diamonds around his head…rubies in his hands and feet
It wasn't the gaudiness of the chain, I'm from New York believe me I've seen worse
It was the contradiction in it itself…so I thought.
How would he feel…? Jesus, knowing everyone walked around with this as their final depiction.
Then I thought what if Jesus was here today, not with all the hoopla and trumpet blowing.
I mean, think about it nobody believed he was who he was then right?
so what would be so different now?
I mean no one knows what he looks like right?
I mean it would be this guy walking around saying he was Jesus, some people would say he was crazy…
some people would believe him
but then everyone would say those people were crazy too
he'd be walking around all humble saying peaceful shit, but no one would trust him
like a musician no one would believe in him.
Till the miracles
first he'd predict future events and they will offer him book deals like Sylvia Brown, of course he won't take 'em…he's Jesus
He already has the highest selling book of all time on the shelf.

Every liquor and wine company would want him to endorse their products with crappy slogans "Hennessy, drink all you want...he'll just make more"
with a picture of Jesus sitting at a bar with his finger in a glass of water.
He'd even walk on water and David Blaine or Chris Angel will come and expose how he did it.
They would even have shows on the History Channel "The Secrets Of Jesus' Miracles Exposed"
He'd be on his expedition to spread the good word and speak against the government and politics.
There would be assignation attempts, he'd stop bullets mid air like Neo in the matrix.
George Lucas or Steven Spielberg would want to put him in a movie
He'd decline
Nike would offer him a sneaker deal...Diddy would try to sign him but...
He's Jesus
TMZ would follow him around
"Is Jesus Christ sleeping with Lady GaGa?"
He'd be on Letterman, Leno
He'd host Saturday Night Live
They would ask him to resurrect historical people
Like George Washington Hitler, Elvis
(oh yeah Elvis ain't dead yet)
After resurrecting Hitler Jews would call him a anti Semite
Go figure
The government will try to kidnap him
either to recruit him
or dissect him
Catholic churches would call him blasphemous for proclaiming he's the son of man
Then everyone would block or drop him as a Facebook friend

Because of his views some would ask him to toss his name into politics
His campaign slogan
"JESUS FOR GOVERNOR...**DO YOU BELIEVE?**"
He would talk about not paying taxes
Telling the rich to give away all they had ...and follow him
He'd lose by a land slide
He'd speak against the music industry
BET
MTV
Hip Hop
Rock Music
yes...even Gospel
They would try to kill him again
His followers would mysteriously began to disappear
They would ship an agent from an unknown organization to infiltrate
Poisoning his food
He'd let it happen of course
Jesus...being Jesus.
I just wonder about that crucifix
I mean if him dying on that cross is his defining moment...**so be it**
Martin Luther King died for a cause too you know
yet he's remembered for a beautiful speech
most people have portraits of him...speaking
Yet Jesus, who only spoke of life eternal for the peace of loving one another
he is only remembered for dying
wonder what he would say
if Jesus was with us

Ummm my brain exploded and I happened to have a pen in my hand when it happened…yup!

THE RE-EDUCATION OF WRITTENINPAIN

We were told those lights that adorned the night were stars
when in truth there is no proof as to what they are
they say the same about our flaming sun
yet how can we be so clear as to what they say
about something that is light years away
just yesterday I was taught Columbus discovered the U.S.A
check the ones who wrote it
and ask them how did Pluto get demoted
saying it's not a planet isn't the disgrace
but who told them it was a planet in the first place
when a hypothetical becomes fact
do we take it as that?
keep in mind he who explained creation
also take responsibility for civilization
they take bones
give it skin
based on carbon dated oxygen
which could run
which could swim
how much it weighed
where it went
hunting patterns
temperaments
an animal no one has seen before
now gets called a dinosaur
some herbivores

some carnivores
forced to accept what they are telling me
plus the dinosaurs aren't here to disagree
but how is it they're still animals that are alive today
that has them boggled in a mystery
just so I'm clear
there are animals you don't see on the ocean floor
yet you are master of a beast you never seen before
pyramids, stone hedge, no clue how it's built
but you can get to mars on a rocket ship?
there are places on earth your foot has never set
but you got maps of mars i bet
they say in god we trust
but is god supplying food to us
are you eating bacon from pigs he's making
how 'bout those Mcburgers
do you know how much cow is really allowed?
you didn't raise it
kill it, nor feed it but you'll eat it
you are what you eat
can be taken but so far
cause if that's the truth
then that's the proof
you don't know what you are
you don't even read these things
you rather them read to you
bible, constitution, declaration of independence too
you don't even know your rights
so take no plight
when they taking right away from you
birth certificate, death certificate
same piece of paper
both certify you as an American slaver
legal tender
worthless to the lender
what makes the dollar?

credit
that means the money is worthless
before you get it
Egyptians and Mayans been to space
so when they tell you otherwise
they lie in your face
these are the same people who teach children every year
and a fat man flies around on reindeer
what's the Indians rendition of the first thanksgiving?
how come there is more decedents of pilgrim's, still living
end result of a massacre
who taught African decedents to hate Africa
the same person who brought
you here as a commodity to sell
same person who brought you Jesus
and he brought you nothing but hell
so to make plain what I'm saying clear
Christians paid for the ships that brought Africans here
this can all be proven
but they much rather
teach you about how fast light is moving
with stolen mathematics
even that can be proven
how did the knights templar change religion
Jesus as God's son
who made that decision
how did Africa and Europe change position?
how could they say Franklin invented electricity?
without telling you what Egyptians used to see
nothing is new under the sun
did Lincoln really end slavery
are we enslaved to economy
land of the free sounds like a con to me
watch what you say

they sensor what you hear
rebel against the machine
likely to disappear
should i pledge allegiance
to a flag my ancestors feared
did you know thirteen
twenty eight day months made a year
someone switched it
as in… mixed it
now twelve, thirty, and thirty one day months
make it clear
that means one month just disappeared
February days switch every four years
don't forget daylight savings time
all of this is just a trip for the mind
add an hour take an hour
the day still has twenty four
you really don't have a sense of time anymore
if they can control time
then what of your mind
void of truth you are forced to believe lies
they tickle your senses and call it stimulation
they package Americanism and call it education
they place masks on devils and offer them for your representation
lies and propaganda stay in circulation
you readily remain fat
why countries approach devastation
you go to church
blessing nothing
given answers so you question nothing
the fibroids in your daughters
the fluoride in your waters
Wi-Fi, 3g network in the sky
do you think this affects your mind?
organized confusion

mental affliction
digital addiction
it's almost senseless
I mean your senses
vision is altered
everything you see has been photo shopped
or digitally altered
taste buds have been lulled by things you can't see
chemical flavors and MSG
your ears appear to be able to decipher what you hear
sounds feel like music from instruments that aren't real
lyrics mumbled yet assumed
actual voices get auto-tuned
aromatics all but cloned
so women can puff fumes and men get col-ogned
who can touch anyone in digital space
touching keys instead of hearts in a digital place
looking at faces
faces never seen
taking humanity from human beings
money orders, checks, debit cards
equal money never seen
a dollar never touched can't amount to much
living in a country where money is printed
how does that get omitted?
how does homelessness get permitted?
killers of dog indicted
killers of blacks acquitted
trick you to into voting for killers of your freedom
but they never admit it
but they conceive
you believe
they told there is no life in space
just earth and the sun
yet they say our sun is a star
so are those lights that adorn the night

when in truth there is no proof as to what they are

Chapter Three

LOVE= SUICIDE

It was love or the lost thereof that motivated me to really start writing "poetry". It's nothing like it, love it's the most conflicting mental disorder in the universe. You want it, yet it has the potential to kill you. It isn't easily understood but the two extremes that exist within it, life altering. A large part of this book is dedicated to the topic of love; both acquisition and love lost. The pain that motivates me is closely related to love that it truly is a large part of who I am. That conflict that exist in love out of love…recovering from love only to dare love again. As humans we function in and out of these grey areas out whole life. Love...love lost…the quest for love… new love, love lost. That's the journey of this chapter, I called it Love=Suicide because it does. When you fall in love, parts of you compromise change. In essence the singular you dies to become part of something else. Or love can leave you feeling dead, lifeless in some cases actually contemplating suicide. These collections of writings are the most personal to me, some of which have never been read before. This chapter captures the very essence of my written pain.

Freewrite love.....

way before I met you
I dreamed of love scenes
so it seems
you're the woman of my dreams
look at me gleam
burst at the seams
I recognize you from my dreams
but never seen
heart and soul
you're placed in between
kiss me
like you miss me
never being without me
engulf me
enclose me
blessed you chose me
hold me
like I'm from you
I'll become u
one
from two
universal
love's dispersal
love meeting love
circuit in one circle
love is blind
your love has me blinded
I still find it
brail love
prisoner of your heart
jail love
put me to the test
never fail love
like your religion

believe in me
lets Lamaze breathe with me
I'll be your baby
you deliver me
come to my crib
live with me
this is synergy
gravity
pulling you into me
this is love infinity
it's no end to me
love you now as I always will
love me to death
I'm yours to be killed

Truth of the matter is I write my best poems when I feel this way…

I live for

these are the moments I live for
when my heart is wrenching
when my hands won't stop shaking
all I can list are the why me's
this is my constant
my soul is always divided
forced to hide it
my company is misery
my laughter is only a echo of joy long gone
I have been betrayed
left behind
led to slaughter
I have been added to nothingness
my screams are a expendable annoyance
nobody loves me the way I need love to want me
I can't swallow
I don't sleep
I toss turns till it burns
I'm not pretending
this is exactly me
when I'm crying
when hell is in my chest
when I see pictures of things I thought I left in my nightmares
only to live a lucid dream
I can't awake from
so I dream of death
hoping that poison particles cascade my next breath
it's now
right now in the moments I wish to die……

these...are the moments I live for
WrittenInPain

NEVER ENDINGZ

I OFTEN SIT AND SORT THROUGH THOUGHTS PERTAINING TO YOU
THE CHERRIES, THE LEMON SLICES
THE MEMORIES THAT MAKE MUSIC FOR ME
THE FUNK, THE BALLOTS, THE DUETS, THE BLUES.
THE RIVER THAT CONTORTED ITS SELF INTO WHITE RAPIDS
ONLY TO END A WATERFALL
OVER AND OVER AND OVER AGAIN I CONTINUOUSLY FELL FOR YOU
HOPING YOUR HEART COULD PARACHUTE ME
FORGETTING I PUNCHED HOLES IN IT
HOW UNGRACEFUL A DECENT INTO THE INEVITABLE
AT THE BOTTOM, BROKEN, BRUISED CLUTCHING FOR LIFE
I'm COMFORTED TO FIND YOU HERE ......WITH ME
ACKNOWLEDGING THE LOWS ARE WORTH THE HIGHS
FOR THE ONLY MEANS OF REACHING HEAVEN IS BUT TO DIE
SO WE KILL EACH OTHER, USING LOVE AS AN ALIBI
WITHIN THE SWEETEST FRUITS THERE ARE PITS
WHICH IS FOR PLEASURE OF THE DELICIOUS
WHICH BELONG IN THE DIRT
ONLY TO SPROUT AND CREATE BRANCHED IN MY MEMORY
DEEPLY ROOTED WITHIN ME
HOW BEING PART OF ME
WHILE APART OF ME
WHEN EVERY KISS CAUSES ME TO REMINISCE
SO I KISS WITH OPEN EYES

REMAINING IN NOW
UNABLE TO SUSTAIN HERE
I REMEMBER YOUR SMILE
IT CAUSES PAIN HERE
LIKE THE SCAR A BURN LEAVES
HURTING NO MORE
STILL INFLICTING
STILL SCREAMING OF LOVES IMPERFECTION
LEAVING A MARK
LIKE THE PRINT OF THE KISS
NEVRE WIPED AWAY
JUST A LOVE SWEPT AWAY
KEPT AWAY....
WITH YESTERDAY...

Remember that relationship you was in that just ended? You not sure how, even if it seemed right then, it feels so wrong now? That song comes on, you see that picture the memories get rolling. The truth is you really do Miss the Magic.

MISS THE MAGIC

Her kiss was enchanting as summers ending
Her smell reminded me of my youth
Her hand in mine made me believe in forever
Her embrace filled me up with everything I had been missing
Her lips sweet as my days of innocence
her eyes reflected my greatest moments
All of them with her
Her voice made time stand still
Still as my heartbeat
Still as the waters we nestled close to
When we would look up at the stars
believing the universe orbited around us
We never called it love
Love is always connected to heartbreak
This was magic
Blaque magic
Blaque beauty
Blaque beautiful
It became silent speaking
The blink of an eye speaking volumes
This was a blind infatuation
As we both lay still
eyes closed
yet still staring at each other
Her face carved in my memory
God I wish she was here
Because I miss the magic

It was her smile
A contagious smile that made me smile
In fact I'm smiling now
Every second away from her is an eternity burning me
I feel her missing me
I miss her too
The way I always have
The way I still do
What I wouldn't give for one more summer stroll
Hands interlocked meaning forever
kissing under blue lights
We use to make birds jealous
How we flew without wings
Magic
I miss it
Seems I always will....

WRITTEN IN PAIN

Adam syndrome
Some pairs are blessed together
some are profound by lies pressed together
some bleed fantasy yet listen for what's true
some people spread they love to everyone but you
it's all noise hard to listen to
when the truth is too hard lies easy to swallow
some guys are all talk
yet shell is hollow
need to know what to use to bait fish
serve as a dish
sometimes we blow words through the fog
only bitches fuck dogs
some do it cause they can
no control of the power in hand
they garbage so they treat people as trash cans
at the end of the story
pure vain glory
some do things for no reason
plotting treason
love turns men heartless
senseless
defenseless
some confuse sex for love
love for lust
lust for trust
that's what eve did
cause him to do what he did
in the end we all Adams
standing in a garden in our birthday suit
waiting for a woman
trade our soul…for a bite of they fruit….

For Dying Butterflies

ENGULF ME
WRAP ME UP IN SENSELESS BLISS
ENTANGLED IN WINGS NOT WORKING
LOOKING FOR PURPOSE
INSIDE, KNOWING ONCE I ESCAPE
I WILL FLY
ALTHOUGH FLIGHT MEANS I'm CLOSER TO DYING
IT IS ALSO WHY I LIVE
WHO WOULDN'T SPEND A LIFE IN THE DIRT
FOR ONE MOMENT OF FLIGHT
IF I'm TO PERISH...MAY IT BE THIS WAY
FLOWERS UNDER MY BELLY
SUN KISSING MY NECK
THIS IS NOT A MERE TWILIGHT
THIS IS FLIGHT
IN THE LIMELIGHT
HERE THERE IS NO DARKNESS
I EMBRACE MY DESTINY
WHICH IS TO BE BEAUTIFUL
AND FLY FREE

WRITTEN FOR THE BUTTERFLY IN US ALL.....

Close enough from nothing.......

It's cold where I am
I sit alone mostly
even surrounded by the ever moving everything
I'm frozen unable to move
So I shudder by the lovers graveyard
the smell of decaying flesh reminds me I'm
alive...barely
sometimes I forget to breathe
my love is manufactured in my mind...not my heart
trying to find what I was robbed of
vigorously I search for my knapsack
feeling voiceless...choice less
my life in the hands of the selfless
the selfish!!
the foolish!!
I find my nap sack
ripped open..empty
my love, my pride,
gone
all that remained were scraps...
realizing I worshiped a false idol
remembering we only live
to die
I feel like the moon every morning smiting the sun
screaming!!!!!
I've lost my voice
and myself
I loved a void
a void that had no love in it
none...
even for itself
how can u obtain value
from the valueless

diamonds are only rocks that glisten
this is me...but my smile missing
where I wish I could be ?
napping under cherry tree
kissing under cherry moons
I pray daily for St. peter
life's a bitch...I don't need her
what I need is to feel free
a heart of gold to rescue me
all I want is a love that's mine
why is that so hard to find
'cause it's a love created in the mind...
It's very cold where i am
I sit alone mostly
even surrounded by the ever moving every thing
I'm frozen
unable to move....

I use to say heartbreak should be a crime, people should go to jail for it. Maybe people would take emotions alit' more seriously. Anyhow I wrote this from the perspective of that body, inside the chalked lines. Dying.

A POEM FROM THE CHALKED LINE

I often wonder if you see me here
If you even know I'm alive
countless times I've watched you step over my lifeless body
always cautious not to splash yourself with blood
My blood, leaking from my bleeding heart
Regretful I ever noticed you
your eyes are my prison
your lies, a checklist from a wish list
who said it was ok for you to smile
like you wanna style and profile at my misery
you never even noticed me fading away from all the photos
you love me in secret
slaying me publicly
I FORGOT MY NAME
so I scribble help in blood puddles
You never could read my script
I've given you all of me
Watching you give yourself away
wondering where or when ill find you
I often wonder if you see me here
Black and Blue
hiding crimson tears
For this is love at its best
you don't ever notice me

you don't even know it's me
But it is
Dying the way I do in my nightmares
clutching at nothing wishing it was you
In my worthlessness I've transformed abuse
into affection
punches for hugs
curses for kisses
I wonder if you even notice me
DYING !!!
melting into a shell of what I never desired to be
mortified at this reflection of myself
horrified by my face in this blood puddle
Decaying
wishing you would love me
or kill me
I often wonder if you see me here

Across The Stars

Alone at the end
treading the entire zodiac
only to find you at the beginning
looking for me
singing solemnly
with a straw in the milky way sipping slowly
its effects contagious
as I sip slipping into intoxication
seeing double
for a second I confuse u for Gemini
but your beauty cannot be replicated
so I focus
on, on a vision of us skinny dipping by the little dipper
into the sea of tranquility
caught in a bliss of foreverness
time moves not here ...not here with u
here the only motion is me towards u
with a force stronger than gravity can provide
I orbit u
searching for reasons to crash land inside u
you are my sun
still pushing towards your core
if I die this way
my life has reason
this is tortured love
trapped at the end of the zodiac
too far to be heard
yet close enough to touch
do the heaven lie?
DO the stars that surround us even exist!!!!
or are they memories
of a marvel long faded
still flickering with hope

like our love once did
does only a black hole remain
where our love use to be
sucking my soul from me?
All that remains is the darkness
that reminds me of your skin
a skin so black
so beautiful
it belongs amongst the stars
amongst the angels
amongst...the God's themselves

The U Piece...Pieces of U.....

YOUR LOVE...
has me constantly THINKING BOUT U
filling me with QUESTIONS...
why the SMILE...distorted DISTRACTIONS WHO IS SHE?
I'm just LEAKING THOUGHTS....FEEL ME
I was FADING AWAY
THE BROKEN HEART...LOVE SHOULD NOT HURT
I'm a victim of UNLOVED LOVE ...CAGED BIRD
held HOSTAGE....DROWNING
but that was BACK THEN
see its COMPLICATED....now
I'm reviling my self
SECURE IN MY NAKEDNESS
Noticing you through SQUINTED EYES
from my VANTAGE POINT
I'm wondering if your heart has SPACE FOR ME
if u can see THE U IN ME
TRUTH BE TOLD
ALL I WANT...is to GET IT IN
my heart is like paper
MAYBE u can u be MY PEN
write about MY PASSION
you have distorted my BRAIN WAVES
stopping me from BOBBIN FOR APPLES at RANDOM
but this TRANSFORMATION
as me screaming your FIRED!!!
to those who digitally grope me
all have been FORGOTTEN EFFORTLESSLY
REALLY TRUTH FROM ME
I'm discovering
HOW DEEP IS UR BEAUTY
do u UNDERSTAND MY DRIVE?
can u hear THE OPENING of my heart

going crazy OVER U
I love u
wanna marry u tonight
since u was NEVER A WEDDING BRIDE
let's do it right
under the moonlight
u in a dress
"more orange than white"
WHAT I FEAR...
is not living long ENOUGH
to love u forever
in time
we can wake up at sunrise
take AFTERNOON NAPS
as for TODAY
I'm looking for u
in my TOMORROW
wanna show u what I'm made of
BEFORE WE MAKE LOVE
u got me crazy
WITH AND WITHOUT you
feeling like...imma DIE WITHOUT U
no I'm not insane
just plain writteninpain

Anyone who has used someone to get someone out of their system can relate to this…
It isn't right and rarely works but it happens. I wrote this from a woman's perspective because it felt like it would hurt more; I was right.

FOR ANY REASON BUT LOVE

if for any reason other than love…
ravish me savagely…
kiss me where I'm lonely at
need not face me to embrace me..
just taste me..
sink teeth deep in me …
with the body shots you keep in me
in my bed
don't sleep with me….
body sweat and cells fusion
my residency is just an illusion
cause I'm twisted into a state of confusion
a place between
orgasms and spasms
conditioned for submission
please no kissing…
I don't want to feel the real of appeal
get swept in my selflessness
fill my emptiness
drill me into a riot…
until the drippings…distract me from my heart ripping
don't stop…
my name is useless
call me shameless
shove yourself down my throat…until I regurgitate the remains of love lost
I'm numb, snatch my hair out by the roots for proof

depreciate me
grab me...have me like you hate me
take it like you raped me
DONT SAY MY NAME THIS AINT ME
take it since my heart was vacated
leave my walls redecorated
make me boil
dig deeper till you reach the oil
use every ounce of your sexual energy
to fuck this man out my memory
PLEASE
don't say you need me
demean me
whisper cunt into my ear
as you squeeze me
I'm so easy
I told him I didn't need him he never believed me
make me feel good !!!
make me feel good !!!
for any reason other than love....

The Departed Art of the Brokenhearted.... (based on a true story)

So you watch... and bare witness to the manifestation of your love, love another
Distorted comprehension... a 6th dimension… truths your truth won't mention
Cancer... it enters the body at a unawares…seeming not even there
Feeding from your continual neglect and self respect
Watch your thoughts...for if impure this creates tumors in the mind
some have gone insane... some rendered blind..
Caution to what you digest or it will be found in the bowel
rank and foul... like love lies that tie you still
As for me…
My cancer is in my heart
Feeding itself from the remnants of the whole
What's left is blackened
Rushing poisonous blood through my structure
Dying from within first
how perverse is reverse death
A body that refuses nor chooses death
Oh how I envy the tortured souls of Sheol
My July is always cold
watching my love, love another
It's similar to execution I'm facing
Lies and manipulation…spark loves creation
Screaming yet only muted by my own soullessness
Heart barely beating
Air so thin I'm barely breathing
Calling for dark forces to embrace me please
Rejected by the land of the living
Dejected by what I believed in

Love
I am a true believer
in fact its existence is self-evident
Just for me...suicide is the equivalent
So...I chose the road less traveled at all cost
FILL ME WITH HATE !!!
Rather deal with loneliness then love lost
When I inhale it's like needles being pressed through my chest..
Watching my love, love another
watch him retrace... my place
watch him experience my taste
savor my flavors
These are my night dreams
My daymares
Watching and I'm right there
Something I worked a lifetime for
So easily given away
By what ruler does he measure to me
Feeling like a savior who sacrificed for nothing
God Damn you ...
How dare you exploit me then abort me
Label me after you disable me
This was not me
This is the death of me
Fighting to stay true to what's left of me
Cancer of the heart
Living is killing me...
who is this me?
Unsure insecure
A heart unable to love anymore
Truly...what is love to me
The flashlight demons use to find me, when misery needs company
So last night I asked misery to hold me
You know I was still lonely?

The time of my life kidnapped
My faith Hijacked...
Watching my love, love another
High insight is 20/20
But love is blind...**ain't that funny**
stripped of pride so very cold on the inside
This morning when I awoke
I prayed that I died
Request denied
hoping I'll have peace on the other **side**
no I'm not afraid to take that ride
living hurts I swear it
love, can you believe I was willing to share it
My eyes are crystal balls
Meaning I see it all
Paradise Rises
kingdoms fall
The bliss in a kiss
eyes closed forgetting i exist
forgetting I exist
forgetting I exist
pouring bleach on our yesterday
Yet the memories still don't go away
they don't go away
they don't go away
they won't go away
Cancer of the heart
Find pieces of it buried in my art
watching my love, love another...

written in pain

ifihadthewordstosaywhatitisireallywantedtosaythisisthewayiwouldsayit

I want to say I love you
but to confine what I feel for you into four letters
my business is words so...I'm aiming to do better
exposing myself to you
thought I knew better
yes...you're sexy
but this is what's after that
beyond...talking till dawning or morning when things in common
turn spiritual bonding...
this is bigger than that
mindless chit chats and
intact zodiacs
way bigger then love
I'm trying to tell you that
in fact.. it's the kind of contact
make the soul react
where sensual minds combine and mingle
make the spine tingle
you're my divine intention
wishing I could elongate my latitude beyond this dimension
did I mention my mission
you and I
stay
forever and a day
what I use to wish away
you kissed away
when you gone I get the blues
I'm not sad...just can't breathe without you
Can't you tell...
when you're gone I can't inhale
does this sound like love to you?

love is an action the heart broken use to do
what I feel for you is oceanic
meaning its depthless
meaning if you submerge yourself in it...it will leave you breathless
I wanna drown in it
Can't swim...just want to float around in it...
this ain't love
they say love is magic
then you find out magic don't exist
it's mostly tricks
this is life..
I life you
meaning only death can pull me apart from you
and I can only die if I'm apart from you
we bonded at the soul
I'm a part of you
only fools fall in love
love sound like a trap
where you fall for the bait
and never get your heart back...
no...we beyond that
beyond what physically attracts
you didn't steal my heart
it's been ransacked
this ain't love
they say love is blind
I see you clearly
get visions and apparitions when you not near me
they say you don't know what you have till it's gone
they were wrong
cause I been right here
treasuring you all along
and if I had the words to say
what it is I really wanted to say
this is what I would say...

but until that day
I LOVE YOU

SHE BE (inspired by true love)

SHE BE
my morning thought when I wake up
I want to be her baker man
I'm trying to get my cake up
she make me levitate
hope the up we never break
hope the up never break
hope we never break up
she give me chills in the morning no make up
SHE BE
sexy when she wake up
when she wake up
she sexy
she wake up sexy
I want to whisper in her ear
wake up sexy
I want to make her breakfast
I want to feed her
I want to feed her
I need her
I need her to feed me
so I feed her me
SHE BE
I tell her I need space
I need space
I need her space
SHE BE
my star
she be my star
so I need her space
I need her star
so I need her space
so I need space...my starlight is her face
I wish on kissing her

even when I'm missing her
throwing my love at her heart
hoping I'm not missing her
I beg her
be my omega
I beg her
be my omega
meaning nothing after you
tell me what I have to do
SHE BE
my problem
sexyx2 + beautiful x damn = she
my problem
SHE BE
no problem for me
no division in me
I don't need sum
SHE BE
the total of everything to me
SHE BE
my spade partner
she my queen of hearts
and when she walk
they want to cut her
but she in my book
so when she walk
I want to run to Boston
SHE BE
my spades partner
can we be two… and a possible
SHE BE
my queen of heart
make me your king
make me your ace
when we get the club
I'll place diamonds in your hand

I said
SHE BE
my spades partner
can we be two.... and a possible
make me your king
make me your ace
and when we get the club
I'LL PLACE DIAMONDS IN YOUR HAND
I won't renege
this ain't about the games we play
boys will be boys
I want to be your man
SHE BE
GOOGLEABLE
iloveyoureverever.com
I want to be a hermaphrodite
I want to be
half man
half she
SHE BE
falling
falling
spellbound
SO
let me type love letters
l
o
v
e

she be

One of them kinda poems

I want my pen to be motivated by whispered words dedicated to me
like my earlobe was a microphone...amplifying the vibrations in my core
I want to wake up being kissed
I want to be afraid to blink cause in that millisecond...she will be missed
I want Shakespearian love...so when she leave I can say things like
"thy love do not tarry to long, for I shall remain breathless until your return"
I want angry...still make me laugh love
two straws one glass love
anything you ask love
love like it's my last love
built to outlast my last love
never put me last love
I want her to paint my nails clear while I sleep even though she knows I hate that shit
I wanna be her crush
I want her smile to make me blush
Eskimo kisses...our noses touch
I want her screen saver to be a picture of us
no...I want to go to an amusement park
and we the loudest couple on the bus
dressed the same, on our t-shirts is a picture of us
I want my money to be missing
I want her to stick her finger in all the pots I'm stirring in the kitchen
I want us to cook together
then argue about who's cooking's better
I want them to envy our kisses
one hour kisses
in the shower kisses

I want to rub her feet to sleep
I want her happy
even when she mad at me
I want us to debate about characters on shows I hate
I want her lips to taste like Hershey
I want her to claim my Jordan jersey
I want to get calls on my cell at times that are rude
then watch her answer with an attitude..
"ummm its 12:30 you gonna have to call him at a more RESPECTABLE time"
I want my pet name to be…YOU MINE
on her mind all the time
everyday like Valentine
I want to make her laugh till she can't breathe
I want us to invite all our friends over
then gossip about them when they leave
I want her to put fruit in my mouth
While I grease her scalp
I want my food in a bowl cold
cause I can't eat till you get home
I want to order food and she eat half my fries
I want us to talk with just eyes
I want to memorize her fumes
text I love you while we in the same room
I want my friends to wonder if she has sisters
I want us to have silly anniversaries
"baby…today makes two years since the first time you said God bless you to me after I sneezed "
I want people to be sick of us
I want to be on an empty couch and she sit on my lap anyway cause that cushion
is just too far away from me
I want her in my mamma kitchen like
"ummm Miss Pain… you know he don't eat that right"
I want lost love to be a blur

I want her to lighten my world so much the sun will envy her
I want her to say…"write me a love poem"
so maybe
just maybe
I could actually write…. one of them kinda poems.

Death Becomes Her

Death…
it comes in many forms
it starts from a distance
slight subtle… persistent
something as golden as hand holding
when that hand you use to hold
turns cold
you don't notice at first
Death…
comes in phases
when endless conversations
become one word answers and phrases
you excuse it
'cause when love lightens your life
you refuse to lose it
Death…
it comes at unawares
shortened and depleted is the time you use to share
but you're the only one that cares
and you're amazed in a maze
trying to figure how did we get there
dressed different then how you left
claiming you just came from work
alcohol on your breath
Death…
it comes with its signs
like you carrying a fragrance that is not mine
or always seeming as if it's something on your mind
or these new hair styles
manicure designs
now you rocking pineapple spray?
new thongs and lingerie
treating me like I'm gay

you looking sexy
but we ain't having sex today
nor tomorrow like yesterday?
but you going out to dance?
in those fucking pants
cause on my life
them FUCKING pants
Death…
it has no consideration
it turns into next room phone conversations
interruption when trying to have your own conversations
you feel life start to erode
cell phones locked with security codes
late night text about sex
you spy cause you love her
you trying to love her
finding receipts for rubbers
Death…
it has no respect
it shows itself as hickeys on a neck
extra hour in the shower
she don't taste the same
she don't fit so snug in your frame
she stumbles and calls you his name
Death…
It's numbing
plus you never see it coming
when her home coming was once an event for you
now you are receiving text from her
never meant for you
you're overwhelmed with pain
yet you remain
you want to hold on
but in truth you're dying
no longer who you use to be

bitter...cold...empty
Dead

I LOVED HER

I loved her
yet what good is love dumped in a void…avoided
love undernourished can't possibly flourish
what good is a sun that wont shine
I loved her
it was like hands pushing a man down in quicksand
I thought it was to help me understand
that wasn't the plan
if love was a house
it trapped me
kidnapped me
raped me
spit me out when the door slapped me
used me abused me
I welcomed that
I slept at loves door
you confused me for a welcome mat
framed in loves name
can you picture that
I gave her
the salvageable parts of me already bombarded by love loss
this knowledge never altered your movements
in fact it mimicked the motions reptiles move with
Gave you the breath of me, almost suffocated
sacrificed the best of me
you took it…
disregarded the rest of me
didn't seem right what was left of me
I gave her
parts of me you don't get back
blowing candles on cakes wishing I never did that
scars heal
yet leave a mark

behind the light its always dark
why do we visit grave sites?
'cause the feeling is almost the same when I write
ashamed cause it always feels the same when I write
it's crazy
murder can be committed...killers remain free
you're abandoned half hearted... a pardon for the guilty
I resent her
she creates new life line
ties to new lives
as the light in me dies
how can something so beautiful
have rotten insides
I say I'm over it
lies
like when I believed your alibis
my trust.. my love.. your impartial allies
it was an act for your show
I'm a great pretender
I resent her
for I could fill volumes with what I choose not to remember
what remains in store...is what hits the core
so before I lay...I pray...to forget a little more
it's no surprise, I rise with the sun
can't believe I was really orbiting a star
that didn't shine like one...
I loved her...

WHATS LEFT

what is left
you watched me love you with all I had
guess I loved you to death
you were an accomplice
what did that accomplish
left my heart tarnished
I didn't even sit down to write this poem
what else is new
subjected to the subject of you
you assassinate my character in open view
what's left
I have written 9,999 poems about my murder
when you feel wronged you try to write it out
mistakes on paper you white it out
life is thicker then paper
mistakes leave dark holes in ya' soul
when you erase it leaves smudges
I didn't even sit down to write this
but every time you feud with my muse
my muse lose
this isn't about love
no matter what you believe
this is about what love robs you of…**when it leaves**
what can a man that's broken achieve
what good is a breath of fresh air
if you can't even breathe
THIS AINT THE POEM I WANTED TO WRITE
but I remember them nights
when I watched you sleep wondering how you were
able to do so
knowing what you knew
(sweet dreams are made of these … who am I to disagree)
If you don't want something

trade it in
give it back
guess you was too greedy for that
maybe I came off too needy for that
forever guess you ain't need me like that
(some of them want to use you... some of them wanna be used by you)
I wanted to write about tomorrow
sun rays and better days
instead...
corpse and dead bodies in my head
pictures that use to be me
I been trying to find my smile
(everybody looking for something)
Now I can't find myself
often having to remind myself
that's me inside myself
in the light
I hide myself
picking my brain
writing is how I remain sane
it's in my sanity I pride myself
so after stain
of love lost once gained
what's left

Love too deep

Fools skinny dip in loves pools
what bliss persist in foolishness
love does not exist
stripped to its fabric
it's just neurons causing static
creating distractions and altered reactions
based placed in physical attractions
this peaks with sex
if good at best
feelings become pronounced
love is confessed with expression
with actions and reactions perceived as obsession
"I've been thinking about you allllllllllll day"
love is the need of the needy to feel whole
subdued by lips to kiss
a hand to hold
yet to proclaim this weakness with sweetness
I have seen men fold under the guise of a woman
disguise of a woman…
hidden secrets… the lies of a woman
because he found love in the eyes of a woman
women crushed under fist
hoping that after the soreness
love exists…
what is this?
loves language will ultimately translate to anguish
or an institution
built to find economic solutions
(now that we found love what are we gonna do… with it)
scream Imperfections at each other
dulled lulled to maintain what has become mundane
this is the insanity of love

captured and bottled inside song lyrics and Disney pictures
pictured perfect
true, flowers grow at the surface
beneath it is worms
the seed of it worthless
yet love is sought out on purpose
love isn't blind
its invisible
a virus putting the heart in critical
abruptly corrupting an individual
love is a veil
a magic spell
a tragic well
you must repel
its evol (evil) cant you tell
love is for losers never loving themselves
looking for partners to partake in distracted misery
companions accompanied till death has its say
love=suicide
parts of yourself get compromised
a strange exchange...just to remain caged
ball...chained
claimed
now you're part of an association
your reality ends
you're brainwashed to believe this is your friend
cabin fever causes delusions
two brains one life
bound for confusion
"who wrote the book on love"
what madness were they thinking of
what madness were they thinking of
its only safe to assume
they too were gassed by loves toxic fumes
the wise man knows to stay dressed to the 9's

fools skinny dipping in loves pools
always drown down by the wayside

I wrote this during poetry month in which you are supposed to write one poem for every day of the month of April, hence the title. I just wrote from the heart on this one.

16 of 30

They form stones forged by reality
pitching them at perfect pictures
these are my dreams
deferred blurred
shattered shards I'm bared from happiness
lovers lane is always lonely
just like liars for friends
destination dead ends
heartbreak season begins
can't get the picture
life broke my lens
kisses feel better in my head
that's where love lives
when it dies
overdosed on love lies
it gets predictable
same picture
hand drawn
edges torn
colors warn
antique is another word for old
how do
you
lose value
love no longer wows you
love don't last past the vows you vowed to
what you once held close
now crowds you

these are my nightmares
pictures where they frame me
false claim's
shame attached to my name
whispered untruths
believed without proof
those that don't know
know all
propaganda and sex sells
that's protocol
are you getting the picture yet
reality ain't hit ya' yet
I'm always moving
not my calling
I was chosen
cool
never frozen
if I'm still
I'm just posing
true I'm camera shy
delete the picture

Mist

She felt like summer
smelled liked spring rain
she would use fingers to stroke away my pain
the world looked beautiful reflected from her eyes
I wanted to live there
counting her lashes
her laugh made me live
her beauty was full
becoming effected by the residual radiance of this
her kiss
reminded me of cannabis
I wanted to pull her into me
and hold it
like secrets
she was mystical
like genie smoke
like evenings in Egypt
comets over lunar eclipse
I wanted to kiss poetry off her lips
word by word
she was saying she wanted to teach me
only if she could keep me
again...I inhaled her
deeply
until she possessed me completely
in her lap...I could smell her
like nectar
sweeter then peach dew
I knew
she tasted sweeter then peaches do
when she spoke to me
it breathed hope to me
hopefully
I will never detox from her

I'm high…
sooo high…
the air is thin
and then
I realize I been sleeping again
It's all pretend
she doesn't exist
evaporated in the midst
of the mist
so it seems
life
is
but
a
dream…..

Smilepin Trigger

It's the smile your hellos trigger
swelling my heart bigger
it's the giggle you produce when I'm trying to be cute
extracting school boy reactions
I can hear you listening to me
like drips my words dropping in to your pooling
curiosity
I wanna be your favorite subject
study me
you voice is flavored with hope and framed pictures of
our future
your my new drug
stick my pinky in to taste it
you're flavored with inspiration
I want our names in the same mentioned sentence
I want to be called
"them"
"they"
"those two"
by everyone who knows you
it's those moments of silence we get lost in
so often
this is when you hear me clearly
can you come near me
I want to breathe what you exhale
when we combine
what happens to time
I know you can read between my lines
I want to listen to purple rain
to take purple breaks
in a purple haze
with purple cupcakes
perhaps I over spoke
yet these are the thoughts you provoke

you are the light
so I need to see you to write
right?
kiss me till we reach the alter
kiss me till we reach forever
I hate sad good byes
so when you say good bye
I try
not to take it as an ending
but the chance to advance
to a new beginning
besides…
you should see the smile your hello triggers
I swear girl…they keep…getting…bigger…

Adams Repatriation

I prayed for her
I prayed for a life mate to make life with
God be praised
she came to me
with me
into me
and it was good
I became her diary pages
she was my treasure chest
blessed...
we became twined
two bodies one heart
moving to the same beat
my thoughts never eluded her
my every action included her
basking in the fact that this is what love life looks like
and it was good
she was my bank of beliefs
I invested my faith in her
"kissed her in her sleep"
every place her foot stepped
Holy ground
I used words to build shrines in her honor
I planted her in fertile soil
watered her with wisdom
pouring myself into her hoping to grow a tree of knowledge
she grew
strong
beautiful...
and it was good
I fought to keep pestilence from corrupting her
for she was the center of my garden
a garden that grew in the center of my world
not being perfect myself

I sharpened by love in perfection
she was my idol
placing her even above God himself
this was my first sin
for so encased in her glory I was
never noticed she allowed a serpent in our garden
didn't realize she was feeding him fruit
how corrupt she had become
down to the marrow
her skin grew cold
her eyes fixed on lust
her tongue forked
and no truth could come from her
instead
only deception spewed from her
the kiss of the devil…**fused in her**
losing her…
her beat off rhythm
its cold
I'm naked
exposed
unblessed
digressed
hole in my chest
what happens next
serpent slithers away with my happiness
the body I use to hold
sold its soul
while my heart got kidnapped
truth of the matter

I just really want my rib back

Lot's wife

Epic fail
watched my love boat set sail
mutiny
the ultimate betrayal
love was a miscarried fetus in the walls of my heart
you raped it in me
scraped it out of me
I'm done...
with the words expressed through loves tongue
lies
if love is a fire
it's too calm
feels just like false alarms
the truth is this pain I bare on my arms
folded hands reciting Psalms
unraveled only to be tossed away
like butterscotch candies
a minuscule fool
ever felt like a microscopic object
lost respect
some place where dust collects
at times they chose to
love you then lose you
scars only scabbed over
life gets rocky
I was dragged over
I write in blood letters
I have turned suicide scribes
to love letters
let me dine in condoned loneliness
the bill never larger than I'm willing to pay
even though I eat the same crap every day
my tip?
don't marry Lots wife

Life will throw you a curve ball…you may really think things are going one way them...BAM! What the fuck happened? You never forget the ones who get away…Nope.

Family Matters

he was captured by her essence
the movements she moved with
he defined her the definition of sexy
no question
he adored her
mi amoured her
wanting only more her
the spacing left him Impatient
her every word left his heart racing
you don't anticipate that moment it elevates
just happens
entrapment these feelings your trapped with
her reflection same as yours
he adored her
mi amoured her
wanting only more her
she became his heart of stones penetration
his creative motivation
his every concentration
she promised him a space
just to kiss her face
so he waits...
knowing she belong to another
it was wrong to
tie her words to the hope he held on to
tight
letting go induced the fear
that he could miss out on something sooo sincere

truth was he loved her
but she had a lover
she convinced him they didn't love one another
however true
in her ear at night
"I just want to be next to you"
she said soon
yet hope in the air
burst like balloons in despair
what do you become when you are desperate for love
a beggar waiting for hand outs
sometimes love don't go how it was planned out
she's having his baby
as her belly grows
their love fades
connections strays
he ponders if it was a faze
season change
things happen for a reason
love comes
when its love season
love life pain..
it's the life we face
it's love we chase..
hmmph…

plus she never got to sit on his face…

MAJESTIC

She has heightened me
I am crowned her magical majesty
she has found something so profound in me
our connection goes flows beyond affection
our context is beyond sex
I vow to keep her
my hearts keeper
I her protector
I vow to protect her
she is a blessing in essence
for when she is near me
I can feel God's presence
this is love
it does not require words
some sounds are profound
like heartbeats
like light streaking across darkness
we need not physical bodies
we are celestial forces
where compassion merges
surges
we are life
free flowing
growing
glowing
like stars
shooting higher
till our desires transpire
my fire is eternal
it can't burn you
for you are the core of it
fan me
so I can produce more of it

we have no time
meaning for a entire forever your mine
less like together
more like combined
oneness
truly it's the universe that done this
help from the spiders on the web which spun this
all love equates to creation
I announce what it is we are creating
a supernova of emotions
so devastating
reality is born from thought
thoughts tractions
create actions
our life is the universal reaction
which means the dreams of love from both you and me
is what crafted us both into each other's reality
we are only two molecules from lions
so I pondered
how does a lion express emotion
he cant
he can't kiss
he can't pick flowers
he can't say…baby, I love you
he can't
however
the lioness knows…
she just knows

How Majestic

Eden

Look…
Everywhere…everyplace…all I see, God's grace
Trees barring God's taste
when I look at you I see God's face
your eyes like nebulas clouds
surrounded by black holes
gaining a hold of me
this love is gravitational
yet sensational
I want to submit to your tenderness
I want to trade secrets dressed as kisses
to the 9's
I want wisdom to marry us
compassion to carry us
love is the seed of life
do you want to be a farmer's wife
I promise I won't use hoes
I craft holy land with my hands
meaning forever blessed every place that you stand
true love must be sacred to save it
can't explain it
It's the way God made it
I see God in you
the day our love was conceived
when you removed bitterness from my tongue
sweetened the air I breathe
your words have taken root in my thoughts
these thoughts are manifesting into blessings
I love you …
this space place you are Queen here
most beautiful thing I have ever seen here
like kissing in the rain
like the way the blue glows in rainbows
not ever questioning where you made the pain go

you said let go
I followed
now my yesterdays feel better then tomorrow
no serpents here
no secrets in our garden
I was once a man
now I have been sharpened in God's image
no rib
you were crafted from my soul
to have
to hold
there is no death
in reference to true loves energy
this means infinity
that means we always was
so shall we always be
I bow before you
kissing feet because I'm thankful
I knocked
you let me in
in the name of all things good
I thank you
all around us God's grace
I look at you
God's face

no man is King
without a Queen

You can love something that kills you. Knowing you're dying yet not wanting to let go. When any glimmer of hope you have of obtaining affection or love makes the suffrage worth it. It's actually depleting you, your very own love numbs you of the pain. I wrote this as a cry for help. I wrote this because I needed to breathe.

This is what I would call a real time poem. When I wrote it I was "write" there in those feelings. Every time I read it I'm placed right there. The reality is this piece is monumental in my life line clearly; it is the defining moment in recognition of the person I was before writing it. And the man I am now.

LOVE = SUICIDE

I am married to hatred
Maybe you don't understand me see
She's like a cigarette I…cant…stop…smoking
Diagnose me with cancer of the soul
As I close my eyes for another drag
Damn I hate you
your eyes reflections
frame my Imperfections
The locks of your hair only there
 to cloak the thoughts of her clouded intentions
 or misguided manipulations
still…
I can't pull away
walk away
Run… away
I'm your prisoner
solitarily confined
with only one hour of free thought
60 minutes to contemplate freedom outside these bars
3600 seconds to post pictures other than ours

the other 23 hours are devoured
by the sound of stone beating iron
chiseling your name in
to what's left of my heart
willfully against my will
your smell only a sedative to sedate me
so I can't feel you hate me
berate me
rape me
so I can't resist the road to hell to take me
you make me to break me
your touch is similar to a dope filled syringe
as you get close I cringe
like a junkie I don't want it I need it
just...
I promise it will be the last time
Just get this monkey off my mind
my back
just...let...me...nod
let me pretend this feels good
maybe I'm a sadist
maybe I shouldn't say this
your love is so close to where my hate is
your lips taste like lies, infidelity
being sucked in by your twisted seduction
distorting my bodily functions
desperately pushing you out of mind
only to find
you...in...my...bones.
call me lefty
look how you left me
you chopped off my arms and leave
forgetting my heart was on that sleeve
asthmatic feel my lungs squeeze
you was the air I breathe
you watched me wheeze

I gave you my time
you needed space
willing I was to share you
70-30 how dare you
80-20, 95-5, 98.2-1.8
I'd take the crumbs off the plate
A doggie bag
with a napkin you had
when I'm inside I feel erased
my apartment swept out
furniture replaced
A stranger in my own home
with you
still alone
your voice is like nails across a chalk board
or a dog whistle
only I can hear you
I'll sit
I'll stay
I'll watch you walk away
try to fetch you
can't catch you
maybe I should just…play…dead
ignore this taste
of you shoveling dirt in my face
no handles
as I attempt to hold on to fossilized love
my pleasures are going extinct
cant panic
went from love boat to titanic
cast away stranded
go ahead rot my bones
collapse my lungs
since you done already fucked my mind up
it's the black in back of me
it captures me

I smile at the sun
it spits back at me
disregarded faculties
and you're the cause actually
your memory it saddens me
like infant funerals
like battered women syndrome
my heart is littered black and blue
snatched it back from you
that's karma in back of you
did I just hand it back to you
strung out
yo-yo me
fling me away
I come back
you sooo know me
now I'm looking for scissors
yellow brick road looking for wizards
trying to find warmth in a blizzard
I'm naked
dehydrated from the inside
this means my bloods dry
I can't even cry
I can't make enough saliva to spit in your face
you have de-energized me
dematerialized me
I'm short a chromosome
that means you have distorted my molecular structure
split me down to the atom
sickled my cells
I'm in a crisis

Love equals suicide

There is so many kinds of syndromes in this country…post traumatic; Post War syndrome. People need concealing, therapy sometimes drugs after going through
extreme situations. Yet break-ups are accepted as just …"one of those things". But everybody don't handle that shit well. In fact some people have lost their complete mind because of loves aftermath. Post Relationship Syndrome.

P.R.S

No one told me
no one made an attempt to show me
the result of loves revolt would render me this lonely
If only I could have gotten a glance in advance
would have never taken that chance to dance
cause when love leaves loneliness becomes enhanced
memories you hold on to all wrong for you
you wish to let go, not sure how to
what you once appreciated now depreciated your value
How-do-you
move along on a road this long
shoulders heavy concrete shoes on
and all the signs in front of you keep you mindful
of what's behind you,
love don't leave
it isn't designed to
Every step you take reminds you of heart break
everything you do
now a wicked game of déjà vu
things you would once peruse
no longer doable
so you avoid that restaurant
the score from that musical

you know
the one you debated
but she loved it so you related
now you hate it
or abuse yourself till the memory faded
in your mind's eye her face dances at side glances
you avoid love looking to take no chances
can't call you stare at the phone
if you did call what would you tell her
that in your dreams you still smell her
your possessions posses you like poltergeist
gifts given traded for your heart in a heist
you can't face it
all the sweaters watches and bracelets
you want it gone no replacements
but tears is all its replaced with
all the years you were graced with
the calendar ever becomes an object of hate
anniversaries and dates for dates
it becomes hard to manage
finding reason to go forward becomes the challenge
calendar filled with hurt days
Valentine birthdays
all the photos you fade in 'em
you wonder why you saving them
you can't save yourself
every time you see her eyes feel your insides melt
look how love fills the frame
now you feel defamed
your body fills with shame
you wonder if she fills the same
she's with another
and you wonder if she even feels the same
night fall enhances it all
owning this loneliness
condoning the loneliness

this leads to drinking
destructive thinking
nothing to stop you
the walls they mock you
shouting love no longer lives here
every corner every chair
her memories there
every place every where her energy's there
you try to replace her
but that isn't fair
it's almost like you see her face every where
no version of love seems to compare
you constantly smell the perfume she wears
you're numb
you go to bed praying tomorrow never comes
but tomorrows come in abundance
and you can't believe she's done this
the radio selections
offer no protection
the songs that made her dance
the theme songs to your romance
the ones that played when making love
making up
breaking up
whenever it plays that aching love
the D.J. is scornful
even he won't warn you
how many ways can you be done wrong
in a love song
what's the point of music
if this make you abuse it
if nothing you do can aid you in the fact
you can't avoid the broken hearted soundtrack
your broken beyond that
can't speak
lost your will to eat

you get the creeps
eyes leak
weak
bleak
denied pride
hollowed insides
I never knew the result of loves revolt would render me
this lonely
no one made an attempt to show me
no one told me

When you rush home to your loved one, but they not there; make it worse you just missed them…you can feel a slight tug of disappointment but you overcome that. And just bask in the memory of them until they return…Ok…maybe It's me.

HAUNTED BY HER SEXY

As I walk in the door I am greeted by the kiss of her scent
dreaming I could wrap my arms around it
dragged in by effervescence
I search for her with deliberate diligence
pineapple body spray her signature fragrance
I part my lips hoping to taste her
she was standing right here
she midget be here
in the kitchen ice cubes crackling
floating in a glass of cranberry juice
half empty
half full
the lip print isn't even dry
parting my lips for a sip hoping to taste her
so much sweeter she is then this
for I am craving her!!
knees weakening crawling down the hallway
the radio was playing track number 3
she was just here
still hearing her voice in the walls
racing to the bathroom
still steamy
like our love making
breathing in deeply in hope of capturing her vapors
the soap is still wet
her washcloth is relentlessly dripping

as if chasing her name by syllables
I stick my tongue out to catch a drip
still missing
like I'm missing her
her lip gloss lays on the sink
naked
I grab it
parting my lips hoping to taste her
kiss her
God I miss her
slowly I open the bedroom door
look at her panties on the floor
enthralled in her jeans
I tremor and fiend
as the aromatic sensation of the smell of them teleports me to realistic
fantastic fantasies
making me part lips hoping to taste her
clutching them still I race to the mirror
hoping I can catch her reflection
I swear that was her I saw in a glimpse
she...she was just here
blessing this mirror with her silhouette
weak now
knees buckled
crawling
dragging to the bed
I can smell her dream
I lay within her incantation
nestling where she once was
shivering
clutching panties
embracing her pillow
stroking it like strands of hair
becoming aroused
needing her here right now

I am extorting
contorting
twisting
afraid to open my eyes
I am haunted by her sexy

Sometimes you are minding your business, love has taught you enough, lessons and you just want to be alone. But here someone comes along and bothers you…goes out of their way to get your attention. And it works, against your will you fall in love with them…but you implore them, beg them, not to take you for granted. And they vow, swear that it will be true they promise you forever. However…

LEFT OVERS

So I told you
I am not a mattress
nor am I a venue
permitting you to release your rage
I was not constructed
for your pleasure
nor am I an extension
of your mother
I am more than
eyes, breasts and thighs
more than something to be
ostracized and objectified
brushed on when passed
or a walking talking ass
to be harassed
I'm not a plan or a strategy
no magic words
make my panties drop magically
I'm not for free
neither is anything you
wish to take from me
I will not be your revenge
for lovers past

I am not a stepping stone
or your ends to a means
your next ex
I am not
yet I handed you keys
to open me slowly
you shared you
I shared me
That's what snared me
nothing prepared me
this is what scared me
so I told you
I don't pawn my heart
and I have no void that needs filling
but I'm willing
decided not to make you
pay the cost of love lost
remembering the first time
you touched me
and I told you no
it wasn't because you
were moving too fast
I just needed to go slow
slow enough to let you seep in
that my beauty ventured
deeper than my skin
although I swore I heard it all before
you left me longing to hear more
now I'm anticipating your poetic words
and song dedications
now those moments
between visits
leaving me Impatient
staying longer
returning sooner
telling myself I don't need you

revealing to you
how bad I want you
kiss me
not as a prelude to sex
just a sample of what's next
yet I'm rushed flushed
filled with confusion
disguised as clarity
so I told you
without words
submitting myself to
your probing hands
admitting my feelings were
strong enough
and a hundred and seven days
were long enough
your words so genuine
wondering my whole life
where you have been
so I relinquish my guard
and let you in
as you went in me
ecstasy says it was meant to be
those neck kisses and wet whispers
repeated as he delivered
mind, body and soul
over-excited
maybe I've forgotten love
because this feels just like it
I do not believe in
love at first sight
but this surely feels like
love tonight
a touch so tender
more so than any other
I choose to remember

and if this is making love
no I am not mistaking love
this feels too real
no way we could fake this love
and I'm in love
so I told you
you proclaimed the same
even in my absence you still in my brain
our correspondence muting life's nonsense
I am a woman so my service
is not subservient
yet I am pleased by your pleasure
so scalp massages
exfoliations, lingerie
fine cuisine
are all parts of my
complete love seen
I'm caught up
captured in a rapture
never read this chapter
ending in happily ever after
so our bodies soar until we crash
feeling like this has to last
so I told you
I want to wake up and hold you
you wanted the same
here we are two years later
this is not the same
no mention of thanks for what I do
far and few those love you too's
no more hugging and soft stroking
now shoving and choking
how could you choke me?
me
you spend more time with the remote
the T.V. than me

your hands
your heart
our bed is cold
this is getting old
you saying I held on too tight
I freed you
now I rarely see you
what used to give me good sensations
has become obligation
and I'm scared
in four months you will be a parent
and it's apparent you are not prepared
I ignore what I'm facing
block out your 3:00am
bathroom conversations
your blatant request for this ass I got
sickens me
as your grunts do
which are only silenced by the sound
of you rolling off of me
cradling your beer to sleep
I am more than eyes, breasts and thighs
more than something to be
ostracized and objectified
nor am I an extension of your mother
I was not constructed for your pleasure
or a venue permitting you
to release your rage
I am not a mattress
and I thought
I told you

CHAPTER FOUR

THAT WAS WRITTENINPAIN

I have an affection for storytelling. I believe that this is some mutant ability I have to conjure stories from reality. A lot of times I'm not sure where they come from. Like I have all these worlds and neighborhoods and people living in my brain. I often eavesdrop on their lives, I know that this was supposed to be a book of "poems" but poems are so closely related to me sometimes I feel like I'm not being creative at all. So I have shared with you a few of my favorite stories from my collection. I do plan on releasing my first complete novel very soon. As for now please feel free to take a peek into the mind of a madman. Enjoy.

SOLOMON'S BEACH

The water was blue
    The moon same hue
        Alone they were
            On a beach built for two

...and as he sat there reading from his book of poems the book he had dedicated to his love she interrupted him.
"You mentioned love and what do you know of it; delight me with its description,"

he mused knowing she was musing.

"Love is what has forged us together my love ....the knot that binds us."

He now reopened the notebook placing fingers in her hair stroking outwardly, he continued the poem with the sound waves make when kissing the beach, his background. His love lying in his lap, eyes closed so that she could taste his words. It would seem they were the only pair in existence . A sight so beautiful one wondered if the stars illustrious display was in their honor. Just as he was about to turn a page she interrupted him, never opening her eyes.

"Well, let us believe love had a depth and this depth could be measured...then how deep would your love exist?"

He took a hand and stroked her cheek..lightly...similar to the way angels kiss babies and whispered, "my love runs deep as the oceans depths...a place where man can't even venture or risk being crushed."

She smiled...her smile, that made him smile; eyes still closed she uttered, "my love runs further, my love digs past the crust into the mantel, located inside the earth's core, burning hot."

He then flipped his page and continued his poem about his love from the book he had dedicated to his love. Mid way she stopped him once more.

"If your love had a weight what would be its measure?"

"Consider the great beast the Whale...the Rhino...even the Elephant," he said. "Add them all together times 50 and my love would weigh even more, and you?", he retorted.

 "Oh my love", she responded. "If Atlas himself tried to carry my love for you, his arms would surly snap."

He looked at her, seeing how delighted she was with herself, smiled and continued to read.

After finishing the poem about his love from the book dedicated to her, he paused.
She tapped him, eyes still closed and said, "please my love, another."
He began his favorite poem about his love...the one titled.."UNDER THEE"
As he began..
"I have a place reserved for thee
　　　nestled close under me
　　　　　　until we feel"....She interrupted him again asking
"What is the value of love?...do you know my love?...My value is greater than all the treasure lost in the 7 seas...more valuable than the riches buried in the tombs of Ciro....even the tombs of Solomon himself!!!"
He now closes his book and places it down next to him, kisses his love on the forehead and whispers ...
"Beloved the value of my love is as such that on the day of judgment when the great architect comes to judge us of our sins..if it is so that he find I but you unworthy of eternal life...I will without hesitation trade my soul for yours....I will find peace burning in eternal fire knowing you are amongst the angels and the saints where you belong...."
She opened her eyes and grabbed the face of her love.."Oh God how I love you so"
He grabbed her hand still attached to his face and replied " No beloved...it is I who loves you"

The water was blue
　　　The moon same hue
　　　　　　Alone they were
　　　　　　　　　On a beach built for two

This is loosely based on reality, I'm ashamed to say. However I thought it made for a good "poem".

One Night Stand

We stagger off the elevator
Heavy grope
Tongue down her throat
All night we barely spoke
Danced all night
Rum and coke
In my truck she rolled the smoke
We blew it down tote for tote
"You sexy" I said that's how the silence broke
Next thing you know my tongue in her throat
We started sexing she still in her coat
No fore play just went for broke
When I wake up feels like I'm being choked
This chick wrapped around my neck like a rope
Took my finger gave her dimple a poke
I asked "you 'bout to go?"
This chick said "NOPE!"
Wanted to get another round in I hope
Checked my erection
Grabbed some protection
Proceeded to show her pussy affection
We fucked the whole morning
Till fucking got boring
Till we got to snoring
I woke up she was kissing my friend
Now he standing...we fucking again
Pussy good can't front
Plus she in her purse rollin' up a blunt
Good sex good weed what more could I want
She said "I don't even know' your name I'm trippin'"

I told her it was Written
She said, hers was "Kitten"
I said you kiddin'
She said yeah "I'm black and Guyanese,
Can u order Chinese"?
I say to myself
How bout I order Chinese ?
Ain't u trying to leave?
Looking at her ass as she walked away
Grabbed my cell order the special of the day
We ate the food watched a movie
I ate her pussy rocked her booty
I woke up from my nap she puffin a spliff
I explained I worked a graveyard shift
I'm leaving in 20 minutes do you need a lift?
She said,"no"
"You go"
I asked "well what are you gonna do"
"Oh I'll probably sit here and wait for u"
I say, "are u SURE ? cause ill drop u home"
She said "I lost my keys and I can't get home
My sister won't pick up her phone"
"I really don't wanna leave you here alone"
She said "I'll be fine" and got in my bed
I left her my keys gave her some bread
I gave her ten dollars she asked for more
Saying she may need some things from the store
I left her a twenty and walked out the door
When I returned the next morning
I saw nothing but thighs
Wrapped in one of my shirts with sleep in her eyes
She look sexy as shit
And I'm stated to rise
She start sucking my dick like my cum is the prize
She swallowed it all didn't cough
Slurping and spitting me off

It's getting me off
I was hard as a diamond
Now she getting me soft
Till I start to drift off
I wake up she sleep
I'm trying not to flip
Don't wanna curse so I bite my lip
I said "I know it's late are u gonna dip?
As in leave, breeze,
Did you reach your sister?
Did u find ya' keys?
she said no, but I'm hungry
Told me order a pizza, hands me some money
Really wanted to tell this chick leave
Till she got on her knees
Then I ordered the pie with extra cheese
She stayed for 5 days
And 3 after those
She left once, came back with clothes
Well she did clean up she can stay a while I suppose
Would you laugh if I told u that was last year
And she still here!!!!!
That's why I'm rocking a baby as I write this poem
Fucking one night stand that never went home.

As a kid I would write sequels and prequels to classic stories. Like how Jack and Jill met. Or Hassan and Ebony the two kids that came to the witches house after Hansel and Gretel. I even had a story about how the three little pigs had been messing with the roof for years. And after the Brick house fiasco he was going to kill himself in the woods until he saw Red Riding Hood skipping by. Then he found purpose. I wrote stuff like that all the time. So this piece was motivated by me wanting to re-write one of my least favorite stories ever. Why? I wish I could tell you. Enjoy.

Leader of the Followers (a story you can read to your children)

Once upon a time there lived a man
who devoted his life to building a prosperous land
where children played freely...men stayed at home and such
no one sat on each other cars
look but don't touch
people didn't gossip or argue too much
It was Important to him that there remained a unity
A bond between neighbors
For a true sense of community
Because of this there were no fights
Joy filled days
Peaceful nights
A place void of true ignorance
silly talk and belligerence
It wasn't odd by sunset to find an empty park
Parents had children home by dark
They would gather for functions

Parties and luncheons
That was before now
Before the rats got in somehow
It may have started as one
Then came another one
before long
this place was infested with them
this weird smell came from them as they attacked residence
now this place was infested with pestilence
from their homes came these sounds
their babies now infested the playgrounds
This man had no clue what to do
cause these rats were doing things he couldn't believe
but no matter what...these rats wouldn't leave
So he asked his wisest men
even they had no clue
for it would be but a boy to tell them what they should do
I hear of a man who can move mountains with words
he opens up his mouth and summons birds
his legend is known throughout the plains
I think they call him Writteinpain
they asked?
what manner of man uses that for a name?
don't know, legend has it he's completely insane
so how can he help us...?
I guess it his words...this is hard to explain
The man stood as to make himself clear
WE HAVE NO TIME FOR THIS JUST GET HIM HERE!!!
well they say the aroma from the burning of green herbs will make him appear
So they burned the herbs and fanned the smoke
after 6 hours they began to lose hope
The rats were in the stores

taking over the schools
turning the children into fools
destroying the property
peeing in pools
then down the road they saw
a man crafted as one they had never seen before
bandanna on his head
he sang when he talked
wrote as he walked
he walked up to the man by passing the others
shook his hand and said...
"what's going on brother?"
the man shook his hand back then tipped his hat
and said my home is overthrown with rats
he smirked and said I'll be right back..
he saw them with tattoos in Japanese on their back
some had words across the ass crack
he saw their children which didn't listen
outside all night without supervision
overwhelmed by the smell of pork coming from their kitchen
he saw them in strip clubs swinging from poles
over exposed in the tightest clothes
he saw cars in chrome and tints where ever he went
food stamp card holders who couldn't pay rent
and barb-b-cues turned to arguments
everyone's lawn looked like the pits
covered with pit bull shit
people sat on stairs benches and folded chairs
and there was weave hair...everywhere
their babies shared fathers
fathers never seen
and when they spoke no one could understand what they mean
no matter how many "knowhatimsayings" the stuck in between

cigar guts littered the streets
talking loud dragging they feet
he came back to the man after seeing all that
and said
"so your infested with the dreaded HOOD RAT"
the man said the hood rat?
he said yes indeed
to survive a stoop and a cell phone is all they need
and they rapidly breed
their kids have kids who can't read
they will stay until your building wont lock
or the couple next door keeps calling the cops
or the market value of your home starts to drop...
THATS WHEN THEY ALL STOPPED
oh what can we do?
he said ohI can get rid of them for you
it may cost you
a pound of your best herbs...maybe a daughter or two
you got it sir whatever you need
he pulled a notebook from his back pack and began to proceed
he went to the highest roof to be heard by all...
then screamed "TO THE WINDOW TO THE WALLL...TIL THE SWEAT DRIP DOWN MY BALLS"
he continued to sing now Lil' Wayne hits
till he saw a crowd of foot draggers with tattooed tits
listen all who can hear my call
I know a place where you are free to piss in the halls
where you can play loud music till it drives people insane
and you can screw your neighbors man... and no one will complain
where you can sleep around and not be considered a tramp
and they will even give you cash for your food stamps
see you don't have to be called whores no more

and it's ok to buy make up from dollar stores
where you can let your kids holler
and you can get a coach bag for 10 dollars
where you can know everybody business
without baring witness
where running from cops is physical fitness
a wonderful place
where dress shoes are Timb's
full of spinning rims
a place where you can all be Little Kim's
a place where all of you can wear the same perfume
and you and your 5 kids can share a one bedroom
where parties on the block
result in someone getting shot
it's ok to have fun with a gun
go head shoot a few shells
if you kill someone no one will tell
come one come all follow me to the sunset
to a wonderful place built for you
called the projects
they looked at each other and began to smile
then followed him…**single file**
they left this place and didn't care
although they had written their names every where
The man jumped up and down getting so hyper
saying thank you sir…my royal pied piper
he stop and said
pied piper I'm not
I'm the hidden prewritten before you jot
I am knowledge unspoken before you acknowledge her
a strength to the weak
the leader of the followers
he took the two daughters before he was done
asked for ID to see they were over 21
he went to the herb man and collected his pound
then marched the rats right out of town

one woman went to the man and said
he is worthy of fame
for the duty of his works...his picture should be framed
please sir tell me his name
his reply....
THAT WAS WRITTEN IN PAIN

GRANDMA

My grandma would feed me breakfast in the morning
eggs bacon homemade biscuits
She would make them the same way her grandmother did
who had learned the recipe from her grandmother...who was born in Africa
when I got tall enough, she would stand me up in a chair and allow me to help her knead the bread
she would tell me stories of the Bible
tell me I was God's child...and not to fear no man.
I must admit...I just wanted them biscuits.
She would paint pictures in my mind
visions of my great grandmother raising chickens
my great grandfather a bootlegger in North Carolina
but...I just wanted them biscuits
so…when they came out…**all you needed was syrup**
while they are still warm so the syrup seeps into the pores
"never bite bread…**break bread like Jesus did**" she would say
but I just wanted them biscuits

so…while I was watching TV...she would say
"I don't like them little rascals...cut that off"
"that damn bugs bunny a evil little thing...cut that off"
my favorite show was "three's company"
lord have mercy I would just want to watch my favorite show
she would come call me...**put me on her lap**
telling me stories of my mother as a little girl
stories of the "mooslums"...as she would call them
and the KING, in reference to Martin Luther King Jr.

she would talk to me about how men use to be and how a lady should act.
"women don't drink from bottles
men don't spit in the street
women don't be outside drunk
don't you piss in no street!!!"
I just wanted to watch TV...truly

Before bed
she would make me get on my knees
fold hands and say
"now I lay me down to sleep
I pray to lord my soul to keep
if I should die before I wake
I PRAY TO LORD MY SOUL TO TAKE
and then I would give thanks to my ancestors
by name
VANNEL
NEBRASKA
ODU
she said this was the bloodline in which I came through but...
I just wanted to go to sleep
My grandma died when I was 9.
but I remember everything she ever said to me
"every closed eye ain't sleep
don't let your left hand know what your right hand doing
same dog bring you a bone will take one from you
grandson better a real enemy than a false friend"

I missed my grandma when she died
but I miss her more now
I miss grandmothers
I didn't realize that before I slept
she was bonding me with the spirits that has guided my lineage

for there is no death in the spirit of life

I didn't understand that her interrupting my television watching
was to keep me grounded in reality
guarding me from those visual lies I was inhaling
as she told me stories of my mother's youth
to put my importance in perspective
sitting me on her lap
bone touching bone
igniting chakras in my souls
evoking my conscious self
for I am an extenuation of their very lives
energy never dies...
I am my great grandmother

so
when I think of eating those biscuits
made the same way my ancestors prepared them
I remember that hot kitchen
drops of my grandmas sweat..only sweetening the batter
I was tasting Africa and didn't even know it
SOUL food indeed.

nowadays... most children are raised by TV's and computer screens
most food they eat comes from sources unknown
most grandmothers are too young to hold any history
for they're children
cooking is a lost art
as is story telling
and it's sad...

and yeah...I miss my grandmama biscuits

A movie called "The Curious Life of Benjamin Buttons" sparked this piece. If you didn't see it, essentially it's about someone being born an old man appearing to get younger as he aged. What stuck out in my mind was in the beginning and ending of our lives we are pretty much the same. What defines us is all the stuff we can cram in the middle.
That's not a lot of time, as I reflected on my own life I realized that that time moves fast. So I wrote this piece to show myself that life is really a circle.

Next Light…

**Head towards the light
It's cold there
It's cold here
my language only anguish
my history forgotten as its created..
I feel elation
like a celebration
bald wrinkled face
not seeing.. so not seeing why
I cry
what am I sucking?
just a lil' bit of warm milk…
I can't control my bowel
just talk to me
hold me…
forget me not
she is my first love
my everything
fragile
toothless
dependent
fighting for independence**

walker
no walker
crawl...demand to stand
jump climb is the plan...
half of yesterday forgotten
birthday party
learning the laws of the land
what burns the hand
will land you in that cage
pacified
I need to work
build buildings with blocks
knocked down once erected
what's it all for
they mock my speech
I correct it
needing less protection
retaining more in mind
those hidden goodies easier to find
not afraid to climb
first day at the office
I feel abandoned
don't leave me here
sad goodbyes
we are followers
she will lead us
my second mother...
letters colors
how to correlate with each other
friendships made for life
graduated
sad goodbyes
the mirror is rearranging me
eyes feel smaller
legs feel longer
I feel stronger

I think I love her
she loves me
we hit each other
scrapped knee bike insurance
insured by nurse mother
first aid... band aid
I love her
wait I love her
different from my mother
we need to discover each other
in love having sex...
are we fucking?
what am I sucking
graduated
sad goodbyes
no ending
new beginnings
in and out of loves revolving doors
I don't want to love no more
oh I never been in love before
she's the one
now another one
two times
three times
sometime first time
a lifetime
got your own crib now
first day at the office
we are followers she will lead us
grids and grafts
colored blocks for stocks
what's it all for?
lifetime friends now faces in passing
has it been that long
does it seem that long
you're married

not fucking
making love
you love her
she cooks she cleans
irons...your second mother
you know you love her
you hit each other
breast sucking no milk
milk?
your second mother
will be a mother
ain't this a mother?
your child 4 years old
ready for preschool then
invited to high school reunion
has it been twenty years
car accident
insurance is a mother
slowing down
wife's endurance is a mother
abandoning a child at the office
sad goodbyes
he's taller than me
vision blurry
my mother getting buried
sad goodbyes
aches in pains
eroded body
baby off to college
sad goodbyes
retirement party
friends going to long goodnights
my wife lost a cancer fight
sad goodbyes
music plays lower
move a lil' slower

no teeth
bold
wrinkled face
walker no walker
trying to walk
they mock my speech
I'm forgetting yesterdays
sad goodbyes
sorry...
uncontrollable bowels
good father
great grand father
fragile
fighting for independence
look at my baby
holding me
talking to me
giving me warm milk
I say mother was my first love
your mother was my first love
goodnight
I'm headed toward the light
no sad goodbyes
graduated
no ending

Don't do drugs kids!

Mary

**I love her
I always have
from our very first kiss
bliss
I didn't even know a love like this could exist
when I met her she was with a bunch of guys
did I mention
she without words captured their attention
it seemed she enlightened them
I swear...I just wanted to know her
she glowed
yet I was way too intimidated to approach her
I...stepped closer
her aroma reminded me of the funk in blues
enchanting...
I wanted her to noticed me...
so I asked...can I hit that?
she only kissed me
this kiss infiltrated my mind
as if engulfed** by the mist of...**of this kiss**
blurred...**in this moment of clarity**
**I didn't want this kiss to end
so I kissed her
again**
and again...
**feel myself ascend
no debate, I relate to her
Wanted her home...alone
with me
so sexy on my sheets
twisted...**

she is breath taking
her kisses intoxicating
I feel her in me…
in my soul
my blood
that was so long ago
yet she is still…still the only woman I **have ever truly loved**
she does not cheat on me
but a love like hers should be shared
I love her
ancient
mystical ways
I always have
from our very first kiss
bliss

I love you Mary Jane…**and u are still, my main thang.**
Over the summer my son and I were trying to set up a rap battle between ourselves. I have never in life lost a rap battle but I must admit …the kid is pretty good. Time and scheduling kept it from happening…yet. But the scenario is what prompted this one
and yes I know I can be extra, but I take my Hip Hop seriously man!

WAY OF THE BLADE

It is the way of things here
a boy glances at the sword with dreams of one day
becoming a warrior
he becomes overwhelmed with stories of glory
lost in dreams based off fables
for some this dream passes with age
for others...destiny
so then if he is chosen
AND ONLY IF...he is chosen...a wise and stern master
will come upon him
it is the way of things here
as he grows older he will learn life lessons
honor
humility
grace
control
all with blade in hand...
his influence will be the very voice of life
his power equal to the thunders cascading from the
heavens
with his hands he will build and construct his
instrument
placing his very soul into breathing steel
he is one with his sword...
not an extension of him...
no, his blade is no different than an arm, or leg.
then the time shall come...
that he shall prove himself now.. greater than the
master
yet he has not proven himself to be a warrior
not until his blade has tasted blood
not until he has proven himself God like with his sword
commander of life and death
it is the way of things here

soon…death is numb to him
as is fear of it
for no man…no man with earth under his feet can rob him of life
his name becomes synonymous with death and pain
many shall avoid him
evermore will meet the end by his will
and for me…
this has always been the way of things
this morning didn't smell the same however
this morning I would face a man who also held no fear of death
young men with swords often wish to become great by extinguishing the legacy preceding them…
it was the way of things here
It is now…
looking in this reflection of a dying man in a puddle of blood
I remember what my master said
"great men do not die sleeping…they die living"
I have truly every day of my life…
lived by the sword
so…this death…is befitting
however…I can't help but remember that little boy
wanting within his every fiber to pick up a blade and be a great warrior
as I now drift into my final rest
prepared to again face my enemies in the hereafter
I smile…
for that man who has just taken my life
is my son….
it is the way of things…here

For Melted Sandcastles

ashamed I was at fact I never knew
blow a kiss into the oceans view
she waves back at you
waters hitting me, kissing me
motivated by its mysteries and histories
my mind a depthless abyss...
sailing upon...lifted tides...I ride in tides rising
drowning regret...keeping hope moist and wet
chasing sunsets...
so I wrote it into the sea shore
see as I'm sure to forget
leaving imprints embedded in soft sands
wishes dreams, un-replied demands
motivating every grain to help me explain
what water reflects from the sky
a serene scene unseen to the naked eye
my appreciation for creation
the yells from sea shells aids in sedation
hoping I dig deep enuff'
making implications of notifications
written timeline
written in a royal design..
my plans race the sands of time
haste only debates the waste of time
yet between water and land lives the divine
see the peace it brings?...building castles with words
crowned king here...giving written words wings
waves bring them into the kingdom
listen to birds sing them
see joy deployed in the joy it brings them
then...footprints faded
forgotten trails of how I made it
castles from sand and how did I make it
waves whisper goodbye...only here to take it

washing it all away...as if never here...
my unmentioned intentions...life's dispositions...
ashamed I was at this fact I never wanted to see
blow a kiss at the ocean she will wave back at me
leaving wet mounds...where my castles use to be.

Third Version

Mind and soul conversion
Speaking in third person
So I get besides myself
Who overstands the plans of the madman
Besides himself
Three days it takes
For thoughts to circulate
It's worth the wait
Facts, fiction, imagination integrate
Third eye vision
Muse on a different frequency
Frequently
Speak to me
Retelling stories I can't forget
So I am forced to retell stories
I can't forget
Forged from an oppressors grip
Pregnant women's' bellies rip
Raped, slaughtered on them ships
So it's no disservice to call me W.I.P
Being as my being is consumed
With my ancestors being whipped
Chained…
The very marrow of my Written Pain

This piece is called Daddy…

Beautiful morning this is!
Stayed over by my girl's house last night
We was playing cards
Drinking conk till the night cracked open
Look at her…**just sleeping just as peaceful**
Clock on the wall say 12:30…
Shit…**and it's a Sunday**
Shudda' done been halfway through Daddy lumber by now
My Daddy is the only colored man in these parts with his own business
Our house was bigger than most white folks house round here
I reckon they never cared for that too much but they sure loved my Daddy clocks.
And it was two hours to the next town to find a decent shoemaker.
My sisters and my cousins would deliver my Mama's pies all over town, they didn't do too bad either.
Not that we needed the Money.
I think Mama like the look on everybody' face getting one of her famous pies.
But even Mama needed money from Daddy to get them oranges and apples and peaches the way she like em'.
Daddy got his money from them shoes and clocks and he couldn't make near one if he ain't have his lumber for the week sawed and shaved.
Better get myself dressed fast, as fast as I can and get to walking by the house.
I creep out the door as to not wake up my baby girl.
I know Daddy gone have my hide.
Can hear him now…

"Boy you 'bout twenty years of age, time you take this life thing serious.
 I'll be too old to run this place in shoo time, you need to straighten up and fly right."
 Wasn't much to argue about…
 My Gran'daddy was born in them slavery times when a colored could have nothing else then what was given to him.
He watched my Gran'daddy shine shoes till he was too old to pop a rag.
My Daddy said he was gonna learn how to make shoes so he ain't never find himself down there shining none.
Found himself hanging around the shoeshine parlors so as when them white folks came around to get them shoes shined he came with two or three brand new
pair, custom made…
Sold like hotcakes on Sunday.
Fore' too long he was taking orders.
By the time he was my age he was already making
clocks for a hobby…
Rich white folks come by, buy a few of those too.
Married my Mama and bought our house and the
land…
Raised me and my three lil' sisters.
Bout ten years ago he and my uncles built the shop from scratch.
That way Daddy ain't have to be traveling every which away to sell his shoes and clocks.
Everybody come drive to him.
He said everybody go where they going with my shoes on they' feet…
ain't nothing left but word of mouth,
I love my Daddy.
Six foot six, Black as coal, Teeth white as Jesus…
He had big hands…

Workman's hands he was sure that he remembered how he got to every cut and nick on his hands.
He said his blood went to every pair of shoes he made.
My Daddy is a proud Man.
I remember when I was a boy, some well to do white Man came into the shop offering my Daddy money to come work for him
My Daddy said… it was more money than the church has.
I remember when I asked him.
How come he didn't take the money?
He said "Son ain't no price on the soul, My Daddy died shining white man's shoes
I will not shame my Daddy by making shoes for him."
I love my Daddy and decided to double my pace, cause' I ain't fitting' to shame my Daddy neither.
I already knew what kind of lumber was needed for clock making.
I knew the lower trunk of the oak tree make the best heels.
Daddy says always charge more for oak heels, they last longer.
Just learning how to make clocks now,
My Daddy say I have a good eye and will be a fine clockmaker. Coming up on the house I could visualize Daddy standing out front,
Arms crossed, how they was whenever he couldn't lay eyes on me
It was close to round 2:00 now and I know he more likely wanna lay more than eyes on me…if that wood ain't done yet!
Coming round the front of the house I don't see Daddy, I see old Mr. Feggan strolling by,
He never cared too much for me,
His daughter's call me well to do colored boy.
I always teased them about their tore up shoes,

It was funny for awhile until his sons burned down my sisters treehouse up by marble hill.
He looking at me all up from under his hat.
I see Mr. Smith, Mr. Smith was a decent enough White man,
used to work for my Daddy some years back
But I guess eventually all the white slave, nigger loving pokes at him caused him to quit on us.
He usually speak more time when he see me but not today.
He just give me a look and go on ahead.
When I get to the work bench there is the wood from Saturday.
All triangles up and ready for shaving and sanding.
I still got to go in the shop to get my sander and my pic saw…
I know Daddy in the shop!
I love my Daddy, But I don't wanna see him right now.
Just want to get this wood done.
When I get inside the shop, Chicken Bob, My Daddy fishing buddy was behind the counter.
Nobody but family go behind the counter.
I figure daddy must be shorthanded…I'm in for it now.
Chicken looked over at me… \"You need to go to your Daddy"
I don't want to see Daddy right now, I got work to do.
I looked up at the sign over the shop's door,
three rules for the shop
also three rules Daddy lived by.
1. Respect this place,
2. I will protect this space
3. If you break what's mine, somebody gonna have to pay.
I shook my head…I love my Daddy.
When I reach the work station, start sanding off that bark I see them Kennedy brothers.

Two weeks ago, Me and Daddy riding back from the everglades bumped into them coming into town.
Jimmy the older of the two, screamed over to Daddy...
"You may want to pull over to the side, Boy".
My Daddy smiled his pretty smile
"Jimmy, I reckoned you losing your sight, you know It ain't the boy steering this here wagon".
Jimmy said to Daddy again...
"Boy pull over to the side, so me and my brother can tend to our matters".
My Daddy looked at me rubbed my head and started whistling,
just the daintiest of tunes.
It was such a dandy tune, I just joined in.
Old Jimmy started his coach and went over to the side...
As we went by he said, "I swear some colored done forgot their place."
My Daddy tipped his hat and said, "I reckon, few of us have...
I see that being a good problem, How about you...?"
I love my Daddy.
But the way Ol' Jimmy Kennedy looked at me now; tipping his hat, winking at me...
"Mighty fine day Son" I reckon it is, my response.
That's when my neighbor son, we call him Corn cause' when we was kids he always chewing on some cob or some kernels, sum then'.
He walk up to me.
"You see your Daddy yet?"
I looked at him, like a fool, Man I ain't trying to see Daddy right now.
He stood there for a spell then headed on back towards his house.
Sun working against me...

So now I take my shirt off "get to that elbow grease" Daddy would say.
I see my cousin Big Earl coming up the way...
We call him Big Earl cause' his Daddy, my uncle Earl wasn't much taller than my Daddy
but he was huge.
Head full of hair, one time he pulled a tree out of the ground with his bare hands.
He walked right up on me.
"You need to go up by the manor to your Daddy... You NEED to GO NOW!".
I looked at Big Earl, he never raised his voice at me, I figured Daddy must have got to him.
"I will go to Daddy when my work is done, go on now Earl."
He stood there for a minute...then left
Mr. Travis and his son walked by.
"Hey there Boy" He shouted. It was no secret Mr. Travis ain't like nothing for no coloreds to do.
Last year he organized all them workers in the town to stop buying my Daddy's shoes and clocks.
Said before long, coloreds be owning everything round here.
It worked for awhile, but good shoes is good shoes.
I'm sure in the twenty years I been living in Rosewood, this the first time he ever said two words to me.
I said must be the end of times...for my po' soul anyway.
That's when my momma called over to me and said
"Son... Go get to your Daddy".
"Ma", I said. "I ain't trying to see Daddy right now".
She said, "Son... Please go get your Daddy now".
I turned away from her without answering, went back to my work place.
Remembering when Daddy first took me fishing, he told me to dig up worms.

He sat in that water four hours and caught six fish,
I didn't even get one worm.
I remember going home, him saying
"Well Boy, If you can't catch a worm, you ain't never gonna catch no fish!".
It was too quiet.
Big earl and Corn were back...
Only now Big Earl was crying.
I never seen Corn talk to Earl.
I never seen Earl crying.
Corn shouted to me, "You need to go to your Daddy!".
I screamed, "I ain't trying to see Daddy, not till I finish."
Big Earl walked over to me real slow,
took the pick axe out of my hand and said to me,
Calmly with tears in his eyes
"Go to your Daddy, Cousin".
My chest burned.
That Florida sun had picked up momentum and I started walking up the hill towards the manor.
As I walked up the hill, none of the good white folks of the town would look at me.
Miss Helen saw me and looked down to the ground.
Mr. Clarence, who sold chickens, turned his face from me too.
Ol' Jake the town Butcher was the only man who was doing as well as my Daddy,
never cared for my Daddy much.
He longed prided himself on being the big man around here.
He stared at me with a cold look in his eyes, my brow was lathered in sweat.
Every nerve in my body...Alive.
My heart felt like it was fixin' to bust.
It was beating so hard, then it seemed to stop.
As I could see an image at the top of the hill of a Man.
Rope around his neck, swinging.

Maybe a friend of Daddy's, maybe Daddy didn't want to leave his friend's side.
As I got closer, I could see the man was stripped naked, except for his shoes.
I could not recognize the face, it had been gun butted so bad.
The hands were chopped clean off
as well as the man parts.
But those shoes…
Those shoes were the first shoes I had ever made
Size 11 1/2 on the left foot and 11 even on the right, my Daddy's shoes
and his blood was all over them.
I looked up into those open eyes,
pulled out my Swiss army knife as Earl boosted me up to cut him out of that tree.
I kissed Daddy, as Earl put him across his shoulders and we headed down the hill.
Now, all the white folks in the town were staring.
Looking,
whispering,
Ms. Helen looking,
Mr. Clarence looking.
Them Kennedy boys looking.
Ol' Jake the town Butcher was looking too…with a smile on his face.
Hope he know, I know ain't nobody got the kind of tools to cut my Daddy's hands clean off but him.
I can't cry,
I won't cry till my Daddy is in the ground.
We walked to where my Momma was standing and laid Daddy on the porch.
The scream that came from my Momma didn't come from her body,
it came from her soul.

Chicken Bob, Corn and Earl comforted Momma and my sisters.
 I went back to the shop and started loading up Daddy's shotgun.
 Wasn't gonna be no Sunday dinner this evening.
 Wasn't gonna be no more smiling by Jake the Butcher.
 Most likely wasn't gonna be no more shoemaking for me neither.
 I'm pretty sure by the night's end, I will be hanging from that same tree
.As I loaded the last shell, I looked up at the sign over the shop door.
Rule number three,
If you break what is mine
Somebody gonna pay.
Well my heart is broken
because I loved my Daddy.
Now somebody gonna have to pay...

Chapter Five

Erotic KingPen

As I got older I realized I love sex, not only did I love sex but I have a completed admiration for the female in all her mysterious mystical ways. I was never one for trying to make sex sound beautiful I just like doing it. It in itself is a very artistic in expression. To be honest sex is my favorite thing to write about because I'm alleys thinking about it anyway. I am not the kind of writer that wants to subdue you with words. I just want to take my pen, and fuck the shit out of you. So this chapter Erotic Kingpen is titled such because I know for a fact there is no better at making you wetter. So enjoy…and ladies I hope it's as good for you as it is for me.

UNTITLED...

THIS HOW IT'S SUPPOSE TO BE
NAKED BODY CLOSE TO ME
WHISPER ITS ONLY YOU FOR ME
WHILE WE HERE MAKE THE MOST OF ME
NEVER SAY NO, JUST TELL ME WHERE
SOAKING WET I DONT CARE
SHAVE SHORT OR FULL OF HAIR
HANDS ON YOUR BACK HIPS IN THE AIR
GRAB MY ASS PULL UP A CHAIR
CANDLE WAX OR TRUTH OR DARE
BLINDFOLDED SUCK MY NECK
SHAME MY BODY COME CORRECT
LETS GET MOIST AND LOSE OUR VOICE
TOP OR BOTTOM ITS UR CHOICE
RENDERED SPEECHLESS
EAT UR PEACHES

SEXY BODY...SEXY FEATURES
FLAIR UR NOSE
CURL YOUR TOES
MESS YA HAIR
LOSE YA CLOTHES
LOOK AT ME
WHISPER SOUNDS
OFF THE BED, HIT THE GROUND
PREETY ASS
NICE AND ROUND
SEXY SECRET
LOST THEN FOUND
TOSS UR PRIDE
 SADDLE RIDE
SUGAR WALL I FEEL INSIDE
CRUSH YA WALLS AGAINST MY STICK
GRIND IT SLOW, POP IT QUICK
LOVE THOSE HIPS
NICE AND THICK
TURN MY SNAKE INTO A BRICK
LICK IT NOW WATCH IT SPIT
ROLL UR EYES, GRAB UR TITS
MAKE IT SPLISH I LOVE THEM SOUNDS
RIDE THE TOP THEN BRING IT DOWN
NO LOVE MAKING LETS JUST POUND
FLESH ON FLESH I LOVE THEM SOUNDS
DOGGIE STYLE BUT STARE ME DOWN
A HOUR IN WONT WEAR ME DOWN
GRAB MY HAIR AND TEAR ME DOWN
A HOUR IN WONT WEAR ME DOWN
LOCK YOUR ANKLES GO TO TOWN
SCREAM ANY NAME IF U DONT KNO IT
NASTY THING PROUD TO SHOW IT
IF YOU NEED SOME MORE ILL GROW IT
YOU GOT ALL THAT ASS SO THROW IT
U A NASTY ASS U KNO IT

PARK THAT ASS SO I CAN TOW IT
FLOAT THAT BOAT SO I CAN ROW IT
SUPERHEAD, YOUR SO HEROIC
HERES MY PASTE DONT LET IT WASTE
OR CRY ABOUT THE AFTER TASTE
SWALLOW IT ALL...GET SOME MORE
SLAP MY FACE U DIRTY WHORE
DONT GIVE IN JUST GIVE ME MORE
CAUSE I WONT STOP UNTIL ITS SORE
YOU DONT WANT ME TO I'M SURE
TURN UP THE TV CLOSE THE DOOR
THAT KITTY KATS ABOUT TO ROAR
MAKE IT RAIN ILL MAKE IT POUR
SHAKEN KNEES CALLING GOD
ASKING WHY MY SHITS SO HARD
LOSE YA MIND GO RETARD
SPREAD YA LEGS DROP YA GUARD
YOU TALKING TONGUES, I GOT U SPRUNG
DOING SHIT U NEVER DONE
HOLD U STILL WATCH U CUM
SIGNIFIES MY JOB IS DONE....

For The Naked

she told me she was addicted to my eroticism
said she liked how I kicked it
and could I exhibit...what I scripted
manuscript it...I flipped it
I said, well my mouth may move when I lick it
so when we visit
no shame when I kiss it
no need to act strange
when the fluids exchange
we elevating to next plains
she started CPR on my candy bar
like its having chest pain's
this shit is suite like presidential
mouth on the head
getting mental
u juggle too?
I'm loving u
she carried on like nothings new
69
is that a challenge?
I prey for u
sink in my talons
I drink women by the gallons
yeah
u saying bad words
backwards
screaming like them porno actors
'cept u ain't faking it
you just no good at taking it
not just my mouth
my whole face in it
your hole has that extra sweet taste in it
suck my tongue
taste the lust in us

take your breast...
push em together
mush em together
let me suck em together
I could fuck 'em forever
yeah...it gets bigger
you chicken?...did I ruffle your feathers?
I'm a beat them cheeks
till u leak
till I make your pussy speak
make you toss out them sheets
they won't be dry till next week
look at me when I'm mounting u
what you think all this humping is amounting to
you coming...yes...and imma bring you where you coming to

Drunk Sex

pardon my staggered swagger
pardon the slurred speech
as long as the words reach
walking in w's
blurred vision I see double you's
lost in lack of inhibitions
lust has fueled all decisions
groping, drunken kisses
losing focus of what this is
I whisper questions
you answer in mantra's
trapped in the zone
where your moans...become rhythmic tones
take me
too drunk to resist
make me
put my face where I never would
make it good
get this wood
put this oak in your throat
both hands around it
I...CAN'T...COPE...
look how you twisting it
mouth wet
like you christened it
reaching for your head
keep missing it
trying to keep my balance is the challenge
can't focus you lucky
so I groan come here and fuck me
you can't hear me
so I scream it clearly
COME HERE AND FUCK ME!!!!!

in a moment of clarity
push past the fruit lips
hit the cherry pit
keigel grip
able hips
off the chair
table flips
lather me with maple drips
hot box
you that Hennessy on the rocks
this that screwdriver
this that Moet
you drunk off me
just don't know yet
hold on
I didn't let go yet
just ordered another round
it's a double
straight
since I see two you's
it's a double date
call me Jack Daniel
can you lock ankles from this angle
can you
ride with no handle
I'm drunk driving
we bound to crash
after you splash
the sweetest hangover I've **ever had…**
written in pain

or did you forget...?

Listen
crown me king of erotic description
the Michelangelo of freaky depictions
sexy poet of the month
did you get your subscription?
pussy fiend
plus I got a swollen ass addiction
nasty poet...never have to ask for licking
licking and sucking ain't nothing...
got my pinky pushing buttons
now we saying something
guaranteed the way I feed
you gonna be spraying something
you speaking in sprung tongues
are you saying something?
press your hands into my locks
mumble don't stop
I'm not
till you get saturated thighs
Stevie wonder eyes
Don't budge
till I get all this vanilla fudge
shhhhh...you gonna lose your voice
got my chin moist
you...you been moist
see...
ain't it like erotic TV when you read me?
Listen
I'm on a mission
I want you to create enough paste
make my whole face glisten
mouth explore ya' back door
no permission
tongue glides tongue strides...ass...pussy insides

you do the addition
shhhhh…this is an oral expedition
you looking ready
my hook is ready…let's go fishing
not yet
he not
finish with your g-spot yet
sheets soaked
like we got wet
make you lose your mind
simple
lips and tongue combine a clit grind
flip thumbs on nipples
simple
juices run…make me show my dimple
smirking cause I know my methods working
nipples perking
light spank on the derriere
got you yanking your own hair
tossing it over there!!!
dear reader…see your reaction
that's my poetic satisfaction
listen
you ready to change positions?
hand me the keys to your ignition?
your fluid pressure…pump my piston?
done with the clit kissin'
we about to get to twistin'
all this good wood
'bout to be missin'
how my snake
got you hissin'?
stroking the way you been wishin'
you said you coming?
is that women's intuition?
you love this bout to rain on it

caramel crooked with that mean vein on it
pussy juice stained on it
nah...don't beg you staying on it
calling Jesus like you praying on it
go head cum...till you numb
like I sprinkled cocaine on it
damn you Tony Montana on a chocolate banana
you doing splits and hip tricks
get this
imma a murder the pussy
and beg for forgiveness
no witness
hey...see we just made love on line sheets
didn't I just get you wet
above this cause I does this
or did you forget????

SKIN

running tongues around nipples like rock center ice skaters...
soft kisses be a good boy...
low whispers
only seven when she touched my
tears from fears racing down my
don't feel good in my own
SKIN
he's not my father he's my mother's husband
you can cut tension with a butter knife
he's going to kill my mother
I keep praying for another life
this only can end in one direction
I keep calling God for protection
but since he won't pay attention
he won't see me push this butcher knife through his mid-section
as the point sunk in
turned my smirk to a grin
I felt the handle touch his
SKIN
how tough is yours
does your pain run deep
seep through your pours
is your sweat drenched in regret
is it smothered in bruises from being knocked around
by loves confusion
the snare make it aware of raised hairs
some can feel it tare
to feel alive some take razors to their
SKIN
one touch
coke rush
get flushed

forget reality
these angles cause painful sexuality
bite my
scratch my
taste my
SKIN
truth as I'm living in
what does yours revile
what lingering inside
you can no longer be concealed
are you a billboard
a temple scribed with hieroglyphic language
is it for art?
do you just enjoy the anguish
me
the pool I was dropped in
I drowned in
the knife that carved me
the reason I'm living
the result of my decisions portrayed through incisions
 the mirror forms my sin
watch me
aging
decaying
the mirror unveils my sin
pain
its printed on my
SKIN

written in pain

RAW

It gets no better
tongue and cheek
flesh on flesh speak
fresh meat
I can smell lust through your pores
and if we depict it
the way I script it
you gonna lose a lot of liquid
I love to lick it
design to grind
take your ass like its mine
use your mouth
blow my mind
fuck that!!!
reckless before breakfast
so get ready to need a cab for work
cause when I'm done you'll need a bath before work
your legs and ass gon' hurt
panties gone
shoes on
slide that thong
ride along
tongue keeps pace
with them swinging nipples in my face
push em together combined in my mouth
sucking two at a time
don't worry when we done I'll help you find your mind
play that hard D
like its NBA finals time
I want it all
till pussy juice leaking off my balls
yeeeeeah
you can't hold back as a fold that
pussy water

I drink some
in your ass
pinky?
thumb?
you say neither
scaredy cat
here's the dick
you scared of that
she said no Papi
did it sloppy
perfect no corrections
polished me till I could see a reflection
soooo I beat her ass with that erection
when I say through that shit at me
it's with much affection
I adjust my bandana and release my aggression
cause I'm a poet she assumed I wasn't a beast when sexing
we stunk up the place like a yeast infection
fuck that
listen to ass slaps
and ass claps
when I'm screwing
I fuck till the pussy ruin
record it send it to your man
so he can improve what he doing
fuck that
pipe down
everybody don't gotta know you getting piped down
now I know how homicide by dick might sound
she grabbing scratching like she in a fight now
fuck that
my foreplay
ain't for play
I get it gushy
call the A.S.P.C.A cause I'm 'bout to kill this pussy

you wanna make love?
by some flowers place pedals in the bathtub
tell your man give you a back rub
round two go make out in the shower
cause whit me all you gonna get is crooked dick for a couple of hours
pussy poked tied up roped
nibbled and choked
you'll be flowing like a river after i row that boat
death strokes
murder he wrote
can I work that throat
what other nasty shit can I provoke?
can I tie a belt round your neck
tongue fight with your clit
and every time you moan
yank it a lil' bit
I like my lip bit
fuck that!!!
bent knees
feet on my chest
both hands on you breast
ass of the edge of the bed
wrapped knuckles in my dreads
we ain't done yet
not till moon set
damn I'm a sucker for ass cheeks
and lips that can't speak
but after I whisper to them watch em leak
we can play bury the cherry
hide the banana
ride my face wearing my bandana
I make them go planters
it ain't bragging
you ain't see how she was jumping on and off my band wagon

if I'm sexy
prove it and sexy me
if its hard
I'm easy
male whore
great for the encore
I can smell lust through your pores
RAW

This was a collaboration I had done with one of my favorite poets, Avel Eddy. It was truly an honor. She changed the way I wrote erotic Poetry.

Graffiti Madness

eyes looked like turn tables...
blending and scratching...
I wanted her base in my face
wanted to taste her 808's
his lips rushed me like open mics
spitting me to be my best verse
I need his master of ceremony
all over my naked recordings...
I wanted to pop and lock
make her head rock
I'd be her D.J.
if I could find a way
to turn on her "Boom Box"
my box is turned
with the flip of your switch
loving how your left hand mixes
my hips to hop
so smooth you sampling
my instrumental tracks
and remix me into new beat box
she was the Gucci link I need on my arm
I wanted her to put me on like Bonita Applebum
she was fresh like pumas no laces
wanted her close like them cyphers in staircases
skin nice & smooth
wanna make it real funky for you
like when ill and al scratched
the basement doors open
had me jammin' like

dub music
he's using that African Muzik
to signifying' the dozens
of his super sperm rolling
my 808 to blow him
love in a message..
"slow down"
on repeat in my mind
as her freestyle spit was nice as mine
i needed my mind under her name buckle
I need to get in her halls and graffiti her walls
till she starts screaming my tag name
I wore him
like old school silver chains
his spit sprayed
my walls with the
heat of his pain...
hieroglyphics on my
rustic bricks
he scribbled his magic
of b-boying vandalism
and then
he wore me like
the madness of Puma sneakers
with Adidas suits...
she don't stop
won't stop
dance break
we sprayed our paint
watching days break
we made murals of art
everywhere...
park benches to train tunnels
we pop and lock
can't stop
won't stop..

can't stop
won't stop
don't stop
won't stop
baby we get down
like old school throw downs
with sexy switch blades
licking under the tongue
going through life
like x clan members
with spray can holsters
we display sultry
hip hop culture
like victims to vultures
where love births
from Dante's peak
and we speak through
graffiti madness

Whatever you want to call it

I need to talk to you
I'm trying to talk you out your panties
such a forgotten art
now not later
nowhere but here
I wanna see your tear drops
from the wear and tear
what, you don't like pain?
what a waste
in fact you got the wrong face below your waist
relax..
cause once I'm in it
this gonna take a minute
not just a minute
well I can make you bust in minutes
I ain't gonna ask whose is it
shit, possession 9 tenths of the law
plus you can't answer with this thang in your jaw
no not here...
fellas may get jealous
but the way you dress keeps hiking is exciting
do me a favor
take off you panties on the escalator...
hand them to me
warm and moist
it's your choice
we can get it poppin'
fuck who ever watching
noooo not fuck who ever watching
who gives a fuck...whoever is watching
my clit touching got you blushing
you can feel that thing pulsing
that's where the blood rushing
I want that

Let's get to my pain shack
I will eat you asshole whole from that back
till it's a puddle in the seats let the driver explain that you wanna smash?
turn around crash ass into me
my stick erase all other dick from your memory
hope you eat your greens
I got a lot of energy
dig at you crazy
till that ass clapping sound like M80's
yeah you a keeper…knees parted pussy farted…arch back a lil deeper
I like what you about…open up when I dive
squeeze when I ease out
you wanna make love…?
ok face to face.. slow kisses
damn that shit feel cashmere coated
look how it choke it while I stroke it
make my whole rod disappear…while I spit a poem in your ear
(your body motivates me to ponder what heaven feels like
just so I can ask the heavenly father if he knew the miracle that this pussy is
you make me wanna go to church ma…)
let me speak in deep tones
using my finger do stroke cheekbones
this is blending
two souls transcending
it's like a trance time bending
ride me
nipples to chest
upright
no bouncing
winding .. grinding.. synchronized timing
you coming

the hips don't lie
look, liquid you down my thigh
you wanna get it in?
my chest to your back
part that ass crack like a sea
coming again...? oh I see
I'll attack
you'll react
beads of sweat on your back
I'll lick it off...I have salty pallet
lick lower...lower...toss your salad
I like to eat buns in abundance
swirling tongue twirling...I know no one's ever done this
calling me nasty shoving my head up your cheeks
gripping ripping the sheets
got a gluttonous appetite
or assetite...damn your ass is tight
slight bite
four finger spank...make my face stank...please
oh yoooooou wanna fuck me?
I knew that
well how you wanna do that.
legs round my waist
my back on a wall...bouncing hair pulling
promise you one fall
just be sure to get it all
it should look like a rainforest under my balls
let me toss you around
you in trouble…
hand prints on that bubble
edge of the bed
I mean only your head on the edge of the bed
rest of you.. I'm stretching you
knock your boots my hand in your roots
ooooh make that snake sound
put your feet on my chest

now cross ankles
feel my dick shaking you
am I gonna cum you asked
no thank you
for asking I'm a spank you
till you thankful
I make you sick
but you know I got midas dick
fuck you
while saying fuck you
till I can feel your knees buckle
but you still begging me…please fuck you
turn around lay flat
one pillow under your belly
yeah I like it like that
look at me in the mirror
so when you dream of getting fucked right…your memory lil' clearer
I am everything I say I am

Freaky Friday

she said she wanted her Friday freaky
so I removed her clothes and chose to speak easy
I free styled my prose from an erotic pose
we started these visual exchanges
similar to mammals locked in cages
I want to shove temper tantrums into you from limbo positions
erect my speech
hold on to
no…molest my every word
the bloom of her flower suggested I had said enough
my scheme is to exceed her dreams
made her stand
just to watch her buckle
I swallowed every acapella from her quivering lips
preaching secrets to me in servitude
I remain bowing to this false idol
so close to falling…in Jesus name
losing her fingers in my thoughts
steering my head…sure to drive her past crazy
crashing into extreme screams
surly we have by passed her dreams
170 licks ago
when I sucked every ounce of discretion out of her
she lost track of volume…
the base from my face made her tremble
she off balance
using my hair to equalize her
words…now sound distorted when she speak hers
she asked could she spit a freestyle on my microphone
now a trip to the lab has just become a collab
she wanted her Friday freaky
introduced her to my pinky
this part gets kinky

she felt me deeply
way past where the portrait of ecstasy use to be
she burning turning into juice for me
her expression stated it all
she needed me to stick it
my foreplay got her ready
just as PRE-dick-TED...
freaky Friday indeed...

69

It's no words needed
It's body language screaming
no matter how you read it
its more than a desire to remove attire
past that
this is after the tension breaks
when saliva is what you thrust for
it sounds nasty...because that's the intention
its breath breathing breaths breathlessly
when panting sounds like chanting
it's clear vision through partially opened eyes
its heart beats increased yet synchronized
parted thighs
its kissing with lost intention
temperatures rising
the affection becomes infectious
fingers frolic freely feeling
gripping groping
then inserted
till obscenities get blurted
fluids get squirted
the mind becomes primordial

request are administered in grunts
licking only savors sweet sweat flavors
lost in it
grinding hip bones result in moans and groans
repetition in volume
increases the volume
this is that place
bodies race to pick up the pace
just to get there
the sound of bed coils foiled
sheets toiled and soiled
a stench is the air
once there
you can't care
you don't feel that ripping at your hair
names are forgotten while you're in the middle of it
replaced with incestuous titles
nothing is off limits while you're in it
get it
tomorrow is only a distraction from tonight's action
tonight...
only one plan
21 positions in a one night stand

More Play

right now right for the picking
she right for the sticking
what she dripping
finger licking
I'd much rather be in her licking
hands in my locks
legs-a-kicking
my face look like i was eating grandmas chicken
trying to taste that paste she spittin'
I eat it like I'm Chinese
feed me kitten
if I shove my tongue in deeper
guaranteed keeper
you sprung
hurricane pains tornado tongue
still licking
I like my face ridden
right on top till the whole face hidden
you not gonna fall?
who…she…kidding
catching shockwaves while she sitting
she said "I cant cum like that"
was scared yet unprepared for it to…
come
like
that
didn't know I could smooth move
in her grooves with my tongue like that
its spring…
shudda' known you'd get sprung like that
don't run
get back
I get a rise from saturated thighs
get comfy

I can take the weight
no matter if you a big girl
I was raised to eat everything on the plate
let me get some
grip that biscuit
more buns
yeah…more gravy
look how much juice you gave me
relax
feed me like a baby
rub sweat off my forehead
then demand more head
I can drink it before you think it
truly
watch me make it drooly
pool me
watch me vacuum your carpet
till u act unruly
truly
I can clean your walls spotless
relax I got this
this just a pretest
I told you before
my foreplay
ain't for play

BLACKBERRY

I wanted to be smothered in her gravy
Lawd save me
trying not to use names in vain
her tongue it runs along my vein
but it gets deeper.. darker
she poured all over me
splurged till I was submerged
I could feel myself melt under her
I was boiling
this fire I had ignited
was no way to fight it
so I dug fingers into her tar…pit
that sweet spot my tar…get
it gets deeper…**darker**
bowling liquids become an elixir
I lick her like toads back
I'm tripping
told her she need two hands to mold that…
instead she used no hands two lips to hold…**that**
swallowing me made her breech it then reach it
she showed the stain
then swallowed all my liquid pain
with no distain
my legs numb as Novocain
but wait…
it ain't over…
it gets deeper…
she swallowed it
then made sure my man followed it
then began to gargle it
it …gets…**darker**
teeth marks scraped along the nape of it
locked jaw no escape from it
her mouth was assaulting me

unsure how much more I could take from it
so I grabbed her by the face
till it sunk done to the base
I told her she was a good girl
when I grabbed her by the ears
force fed her till her eyes started to tear...
it gets deeper...**darker**
I extracted the measure of me from her esophagus
she wanted me to indoctrinate her in the full girth of my pain
indeed I wanted to churn her coca
until we made butter
yet I was thirsty for her Hershey
Lawd have mercy
she wetter then water
mouth waters
wanted to taste not waste a drop of juice she produce
tongues loose
she taste like frosting
flavors I could get lost in
she spilling so often
taste like milk chocolate
skin like silk chocolate
her insides began to perspire with desire
it gets deeper...**darker**
I entered her with no precaution
from the rear
talking in her ear
"damn its juicy"
she whispered..."juice me"
so...
I let it roam in her catacombs...**till it started to foam**
her cheeks constricting from this wood whipping
I mean this good W.I.P in
look
her paste

all over the place
what I provide got her trying to hide her sex face
I switch pace
long stroke
fast
back to slow
short quick
then switch
she peaked
then leaked on every inch
deeper
got a finger in her back room
move my broom stick
get to sucking like a vacuum
darker
candle light gone
just breath
panting chanting
whatever nasty deeds left
I told her
drinking her was necessary
the sweeter the juice
the darker the berry
told her turn that chocolate cake back to me
so I could Willy Wonka her factory
I drank it straight like a daiquiri
I like my coffee black you see
the cream is cumming
her cup runneth over
and over
and over
and…
mocha
I made her tootsie roll…**over**
we became shadows
hushed by sweat against flesh

sounds like rain drops…
I don't stop
not till her legs still
not until she had her fill
even then
she will whisper "pain"
I say yes
she looks
oh Lawd
not meaning to use his name in vain
but when I finish with her
she gonna need a cane
word

Sacrilegious

so she whispered to me
I have given myself unto my lord and savior
I am saving my structure for a holy man…who will marry me
and at the appropriate hour we will consummate our union.
I leaned into her
for some reason she reminded me of eve.
I asked…why would you fast from pleasure?
If all that he has made is good
her eyes danced…I knew she was not pure
the word pleasure caused ambers to emerge from her lids
I inquired further…are you merely punishing yourself for casting pearls to swine
I like you a lot…she said, and I very much enjoy your company but…
"but what" I interrupted…
you are by no means a holy man
I was now close enough to her that no visible space remained between us
the back of my hand fanning her cheek…I leaned towards her
kissed her before she could speak
I tongue tied her…writing poems inside her mouth
my hands began to read her body like a blind man
The first button was removed at her unawares
as to the second…
"stop…" she muttered as she removed her bottom lip from mine
clutching to my wrist like life lines
I…I can't do this…God is watching
I slid my face between her thighs…"he's always watching"

her sundress now above her thighs
she looked at me...**tears in her eyes**...
"**please...don't**" I made a vow...
our eyes locked
on my stomach I slithered
closer...
close enough to smell her holiest of holies
I could smell her fear
her desire
I could feel the heat from her sacred place...**against my face**...
I laid my head against her stomach
a thousand fantasies glazed my mind
then I felt her fingers in my hair
I knew she was mine
I rose my head...and said
"and if a man is thirsty are you not to provide him with drink?"
sliding my head further down her body
for some reason I was reminded of a serpent in a garden
before she could respond
I had already pressed my mouth against her undergarment
and began speaking in tongue
it was as if all the air in the room was sucked into her lungs
"please stop " she said
rubbing the back of her head
I saturated her panties with every word she never heard
pressing deep against her gate keeper
she began to clutch at herself
I pounced at her nipples
I swore she whispered thank you Jesus
maybe I'm wrong
no really...**maybe I'm wrong**

she kept saying things like "no"… "I can't do this"
I snatched the crucifix from her neck
with all due respect…
she's rubbing her breast
I slid down her chest
her flower in full bloom
I'm wrong…
but I want her to remove her thongs
so I eat her candy while they are still on
she slides to one side
now I'm turned on
she tasted like milk and honey
this tempts me
feeding frenzy
till she empty
I wanted to extract Psalms out of her
she began moaning for her savior to save her
but the way I gorged on her manna it didn't matter
it was now…
I exposed my rod
she woke from her trance
grabbed my pants
"I can keep my vow…I still have a chance"
yet her mouth told truth from her souls desires
her body called them both liars
I could tell she wanted to submit
so I pressed it against her gate a bit
it parted like red seas
I pushed into her promise land
hallelujah she screamed…
in pain she trust
grabbing my locks
with Delilah's lust
my plan was to defile her in every way possible
I fed her my flesh like an apostle
she flowing Nile rivers

moaning begging God to forgive her
it got so sodomistic I felt like Lot
plus she came a lot
I was in it all (k)night ...like Camelot
she didn't understand
she was waiting for me to cum again
like the son of man

-beware of he with a serpents tongue
he will get to eating ya' forbidden fruits

and leave your ass sprung...

METHODS

My methods are working
I know this for certain
to think this all started from flirting
kissing and touching
pushing your buttons
till speaking turns leaking and gushing
fingers that linger cause fluids to rush in
your sounds astound yet cause no interruptions
the way you spilling is like an eruption
all I triggered are bodily functions
loving the way that I am rubbing
I can tell the way you say that your cumming
my methods are working
I know this for certain
your nipples are perking
to the sounds of me slurping
sucking, you twisting and bucking
mumbling something
calling your savor
as I bask in your flavor
filling my flask with your flavor
sipping while your tripping
then ask me your flavor
I would pay cash for your flavor
you can cum now
and thank me later
my methods are working
I know this for certain
your referring to yourself in third person
oozing and squirting
moving and twerking
mashing and crashing
you need this to happen
folding like them covers you holding

hips rolling
lips swollen
releasing sounds you can't hold in
as I go in
I can feel your river flowing
follow the drip
I mean drop
meaning it don't stop
won't stop
meaning my metal pushed past
the bloom on your rose petals
can you see my scepter
releasing your nectar
scream it gets no better than this
wetter than this
your neighbors envious
my methods are working
I know this for certain
you twisting and jerking
I know nothings hurting
digging in your grounds
where orgasms lurking
you flipping and kicking
I'm constantly sticking
your fruit ripe
right for the picking
this night you tight while I'm sticking
you flipping and dripping
fighting, biting lips in
you humming and cumming
fighting and running
breaking and shaking
giving and taking
I know you ain't faking
cause my methods are working
I know this for certain

'cause the show ain't over
and you done pulled down the curtain

EROTIC KINGPEN

It matters not if you know me
you know what I'm capable of
my reputation speaks for itself
I send the sensual intellectuals on trips
with my erotic manuscripts
not to tease you
too brief to please you
see if we are going to make a world premiere
this is just a preview
for me this is more than poetic rhymes
it's a blueprint of how I do when it is doing time
what I do with the body I do with the mind
fuck it up
see I cram to make you understand
exactly where you are cumming from
don't you see the heat I provoke with my quotes
it's like long strong strokes
naughty poet spank me
feed me your panties
till they melt in my mouth like cotton candy
toes curled
tongue sweet as cinnamon swirls
you like the way my tongue twirls
eating the oyster till I find the pearl
feminine fluids
I'm a fiend
now if there is any better at getting you wetter
that remains to be seen
who causes verbal extractions
making you cross ankles
vaginal contractions
that's just a normal reaction
project my speech till you reach satisfaction
breach climaxing

I'm known for ass taxing
pussy waxing
dick slashing
till it's splashing
inches causing flinches
cringes
I'm giving you the business
get this
stop denying you dying to hit this…**fiend**
if there is any better at getting you wetter
that remains to be seen
my tongue will double cross you
clit torture
watch me turn salad tosser
you say you don't like it till
I've done it
I lick it
they love it
in fact I make them love
everything I am capable of
kissing toes in bubble bath tubs
visualize with open eyes
me kissing inner thighs
looking in her eyes
my poetry is the literal equivalent
to having sex with me
let me describe it
I introduce you to my privates
feels psychotic when I'm inside it
you like it rough
I'll pile drive it
two pillows under your stomach
makes it more equipped for me to ride it
king of erotics
you know what I mean
if there is any better

at getting you wetter
that remains to be seen
talking about after the splash
us kissing in the aftermath
in the morning moist sheets
sun streaks across your cheek
kiss lips
want to know how your sleep taste
mount you
see if you could keep pace
sweeping locks out your face
I am sex
you claim you cumming
we nowhere near yet
didn't even pull your hair yet
didn't go from the dresser to the chair yet
you didn't super soak my double dare yet
we cooking
get your hair net
ripping fishnets
handle this
sit on it
you won't stand for this
moaning over prince singing scandalous
you know what that means
if there is any better
at getting you wetter
that remains to be seen
my tongue win championships
are you on my team?
Don't cuss or scream
keep it clean
clean as them sugar walls
I lick between
It's not too many thighs I fit between
but I'll rev up your dick machine

I said it
if there is a freakier pen than mine
go and get it
I'm a beast
last week I got a girl pregnant
with a piece
got you popping like chicken grease
with the seasoning in it
feels good when he's in it
this beautiful dick
got white sands and palm trees in it
you a freestyle poem when I script ya'
shouting orders in a whisper
are you a good listener?
squeeze me
you can cum now
it's easy
follow me
I'm cumming too
swallow me
by now I'm sure you see what I mean
now if there is any better
at getting you wetter
that remains to be seen

THAT WAS WRITTENINPAIN

Printed in Germany
by Amazon Distribution
GmbH, Leipzig